'Organisational culture's built through words and actions. This book shows you the *conversations* you need to spark the *behaviour* you want to create the *culture* you desire.'

Michael Bungay Stanier, bestselling author of *The Coaching Habit* and *How to Begin*

'In *Let's Talk Culture*, Shane manages to do what many culture experts cannot: simplify the complexity that is culture. Full of stories and insights, Shane unpacks the five conversations about culture that every leader should have with their team. This book is a must-read for anyone who wants to create a culture worth belonging to.'

Gabrielle Dolan, International keynote speaker and bestselling author of six books, including *Magnetic Stories* and *Stories for Work*

'Although leaders intuitively know that culture is key to the success of their organisations and the wellbeing of their employees, it is a notoriously slippery construct. Shane helps leaders gain traction by distilling a broad set of research findings and ideas into compelling frameworks, providing concrete examples of practices others have followed, and offering practical advice for putting the ideas into action. I would highly recommend this book to any leader embarking on a large-scale program of culture change.'

Sameer B. Srivastava, Associate Professor and Ewald T. Grether Chair in Business Administration and Public Policy at UC Berkeley's Haas School of Business, University of California; Co-director Berkeley Culture Initiative

'Shane has done a great job in demystifying and making the case for the role of a people leader in defining, building, changing, and strengthening culture. This book is full of practical questions and actions all leaders should be asking themselves and their teams.'

Steph Clarke, facilitator; host of *Steph's Business Bookshelf* podcast

'It's true that the best storytelling wins, but the leader who knows how to talk about culture helps the entire team win. In this engaging and entertaining book, Shane has crafted the roadmap for exactly how to have those critical conversations that will help you craft the kinds of culture everyone is taking about. I wish I'd had this book when I started my managerial journey 20 years ago. If you're charged with managing others, this book is the companion you've been looking for.'

Mike Ganino, Public speaking and storytelling coach; creator of The Mike Drop Moment

'Great stuff from Shane, who not only decodes culture, but also provides the data that senior managers require to fund its investment of time and money and the practical insights necessary to do it well, every time.'

Colin D. Ellis, international speaker, culture change facilitator
and author of *Culture Hacks*

'After over 20 years running my recruitment business, speaking to different organisations daily about the highs and lows of leading people, I can't express enough the impact culture has on the success of an organisation and the overall job satisfaction of people who work there. What I love about Shane's book is he really gets to the heart of what drives culture and, through learning from some of the best places to work in Australia, shares with us some of the key actions leaders can take to influence and shape the culture they aspire to. Most of what I have learnt as a leader has been through trial and error and many years of experience; I wish I had read this book earlier in my career.'

Nikki Beaumont, Founder and CEO of Beaumont People

'As a leader, how do you comprehend something you can see, feel and experience every day, yet struggle to explain to anyone outside of it? You have a conversation. Many conversations. *Let's Talk Culture* provides the conversations every leader who wants to be intentional about culture must first have with themselves. Shane skilfully weaves hundreds of impressions together and casually yet pragmatically offers the blueprint to growing a culture that lives, is inclusive, and wins.'

James Comer, Head of People and Communities, Australia and New Zealand, Cisco

'Loved, loved, loved this book. Insightful, instructive, and inspiring, Shane has once again delivered a game-changing book, perfect for anyone, at any level, in any organisation, who wants to play their part in unlocking a culture that enables others to be their brilliant selves.'

Janine Garner, international speaker, three-time bestselling author, CEO of Curious Minds AUS Pty Ltd, and host of the *Unleashing Brilliance* podcast

'Shane paints a wonderfully vivid narrative of culture as a language we can all learn to speak, even if our dialects are slightly different. As the leader of an integrated health system, this book will aid me in building a more inclusive team to better care for the increasingly diverse communities we serve.'

Tracy Michael, senior healthcare executive

LET'S TALK CULTURE

LET'S TALK

CULTURE

SHANE MICHAEL HATTON

MAJOR
STREET

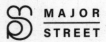 First published in 2022 by Major Street Publishing Pty Ltd
info@majorstreet.com.au | +61 421 707 983 | majorstreet.com.au

 A catalogue record for this book is available
from the National Library of Australia

Printed book ISBN: 978-1-922611-38-3
Ebook ISBN: 978-1-922611-39-0

Cover design by Avenir Creative House
Internal design by Production Works
Printed in Australia by IVE Group, an Accredited ISO AS/NZS 14001:2004
Environmental Management System Printer.

10 9 8 7 6 5 4 3 2 1

Contents

Preface   ix

Part One: A conversation about culture   **1**

Chapter 1   We're all a little different
Celebrate your uniqueness   3

Chapter 2   The unseen advantage
Get clear on your purpose   17

Chapter 3   The problem with culture
Remove your roadblocks   29

Chapter 4   The conversations before the conversations
Start with your foundations   51

Part Two: Culture conversations   **65**

Chapter 5   The expectation conversation
Make the unspoken spoken   67

Chapter 6   The clarification conversation
Make the invisible observable   87

Chapter 7   The communication conversation
Make the words a language   107

Chapter 8   Pick three and make it easy to see
Focus on what matters most   129

Part Three: Keeping the conversation going   139

Chapter 9   The confrontation conversation
Make feedback less difficult   143

Chapter 10   The celebration conversation
Make recognition more meaningful   161

Chapter 11   The dark side of culture
Don't accidentally build a cult   181

Chapter 12   The path forward
Become a Culture Champion   197

A final summary
Reinforce what you've learned   215

Say it again   221

About the author   223

Acknowledgements   225

References   227

Index   237

Preface

Brace yourself for a wild ride of emotions.

If I could go back and speak to myself as I was setting out to write a book on culture, that's what I would say. Not because I expected that writing this book would be easy. It's more that I underestimated how hard it would be.

I'll explain. There's this popular story about three goldfish that you might be familiar with. It was part of a commencement speech delivered by David Foster Wallace in 2005 at Kenyon College, later published as an essay titled 'This Is Water', and it quickly became one of his most read pieces of work. The story goes:

> 'There are these two young fish swimming along, and they happen to meet an older fish swimming the other way, who nods at them and says, "Morning, boys. How's the water?" And the two young fish swim on for a bit, and then eventually one of them looks over at the other and goes, "What the hell is water?"'

Writing a book about culture feels kind of like a goldfish writing a book about water. We spend our lives immersed in it but remain mostly unaware of its presence or impact.

I didn't grow up in a particularly religious family, but my mother is a teacher's aide at an Anglican school, so the limited experience of religion I did have in my younger years typically revolved around that.

I'll never forget the time as a young teen when I swore at church and was met by the full weight of an older lady's eyes on me. She didn't say a word, but she really didn't have to. In her defence she was actually a very kind person, but I knew in that moment I had done something that wasn't part of the culture there.

When I was at university, I picked up a casual job in the warehouse of a surf clothing store. We stood all day around a long workbench scanning items of clothing to be distributed to different stores and throwing them into numbered boxes that correlated with the store numbers. Once each box was full, we would tape it up and ship it to the store and start the process over. Very few people I knew there liked the job, but it wasn't because the work was mundane and repetitive. It was because the warehouse manager had a very strict 'no talking while working' rule. I mean, not a single non-work-related word was to be spoken. It was a policy he seemed to find enjoyment in enforcing. For eight hours a day, we stood around the desk listening to the repetitive beeps of a scanner. (I can still hear them when I go to sleep at night.) It was one of my earliest recollections of hearing someone talk about hating the culture.

I remember starting my career working in local government. My role was to coach local community groups on how to run better public events. I didn't realise how different this world of work would be to anything I had experienced in the past: an oddly specific number of minutes for lunch, forms for absolutely everything and meetings about meetings that seemed to include every person or department you could think of. Nobody really questioned why; it was just the way things were done around there. It's one of the first times I remember having to make a decision about whether that was a culture I wanted to be part of.

When I look back now, I can spot culture everywhere. Like that bit of food in a friend's teeth you should have told them about earlier but now you've missed the window and you can't stop looking at it, culture becomes hard to unsee once you're aware of it. But most of the time, culture was all about me. It informed what I could get away with and what I couldn't. It was just a word I used to describe an environment I loved or hated. That's it. I never questioned what it was all about, why it mattered, how it worked or even necessarily the part I played in it. I never had to. Until I stepped into leadership for the first time and my boss told me, 'You're now responsible for the culture here'.

Responsible?! I wasn't even sure I knew what it was.

My best guess is that this has been your experience, too. You've spent most of your career as a goldfish swimming and now, all of a sudden, you're being asked to make sense of the water. You know culture is important but you're still figuring out exactly what it is, how it helps, what it's for and how (or if) you can influence it.

I don't think learning about culture is difficult because there is a lack of information; it's quite the opposite. There has been so much written to try and make sense of it that it can feel a little overwhelming.

Make no mistake, culture is complex, but it doesn't need to be complicated. I wrote this book because it's the book I wish I'd had when my manager told me to take responsibility for the culture.

If you've picked up this book, I can imagine you find yourself in a similar place:

- You want some help to make sense of what culture is all about.
- You want to shape a team that people love to be a part of.
- You want to shape an environment that people love to work in.
- You want a team you love to lead.
- You want a team that feels like it is aligned and moving forward together.
- You want the practical skills to develop a strategy for your culture.
- You want a culture that helps you achieve results.

If this sounds like you, then this book contains the conversations you'll need.

Intent before content

In my previous book, *Lead the Room: Communicate a Message That Counts in Moments That Matter*, I wrote about the importance of intent before content and getting clear on what matters most. So, before we get started, it's important we get clear on who I wrote this book for and why.

My intention for this book is that it will quickly become your 'go-to how-to' for building the team culture you want.

This book won't show you how to build a 'healthy' team culture because 'healthy' is not for me to define for you. I know some organisations that require their staff to be available 24/7 and others that wouldn't dare contact an employee on their day off. If you talk to people from both organisations, they would both describe that as a normal or 'healthy' part of their culture. The team you want and the culture you choose to lead and shape is entirely up to you; this book is here to provide the framework and tools to enable it.

About our research

Experience has taught me that if you want a book to be helpful and memorable, it needs to be simple. But if you're going to tackle a book on a huge and complex topic like *culture*, you want to know that it's thorough. If culture can influence – and some might even say determine – the success of a team, then it's important to clearly understand as much as you can about it.

I wanted to know what people like you think about culture. What it means to you. How you define it. How you view your role in building and shaping it. Where you feel confident and where you feel stuck.

Sometimes the most obvious solution is the best. So, I took the time to ask.

I'm not an academic and I'm not a researcher, but I am deeply curious and a learner by nature. I love taking big, complex ideas and finding ways to make them accessible to the everyday leader. So, in 2021 I engaged McCrindle Research, an Australian research company with specialist skills in collecting and analysing data and demographics, to bring research to life to help me explore the attitudes and experiences around team culture for people leaders.

We set out with a few key research objectives for people leaders, including to:

· explore their understanding of what culture is
· gain insights into their beliefs about their role in shaping culture
· investigate what builds and what detracts from culture
· understand how equipped they feel to influence culture within their organisation.

This book draws on the findings from our quantitative study of 1002 managers from across Australia, along with a series of in-depth qualitative interviews with managers at some of Australia's best places to work. To help you better understand the sampling of people leaders, we applied the following criteria to participants:

· Age: 18+
· Location: Australia
· Employment status: Full-time
· Company size: 20 or more employees
· Current role: Described as middle manager, team leader or people leader
· Team size: At least two people directly report to them.

This book is for you

Positioned right in the middle of the organisational chart, managing relationships on all sides, you've got leaders looking to you for outcomes, colleagues looking to you for support and a team looking to you for answers. You're in the engine room of the business, managing the day-to-day problems and tensions, dealing with decisions flowing down the line and daily pressure coming up it. It can often feel like your position means you have limited control or authority, but I want to remind you that your influence is significant.

I understand the pressure of moving from being a technical expert at the top of your game to carrying the responsibility of leading people, and maybe even leading leaders. I've been you and I see you. I wrote this book for you.

You'll likely find yourself in one of three places right now:

1. **You're an aspiring people leader.** You're not leading people yet but you're putting in the work. You've got your sights set on leadership, and you want to build the confidence and capability you'll need when you get there. You might not be leading people yet, but leading under a leader makes you no less of a leader. Read this book to help yourself hit the ground running.
2. **You're a new people leader.** You're transitioning from individual to collective, from 'I' to 'we'. You know it's not just about you anymore, and you're ready to build a thriving and cohesive team. You're leading people and you understand the important role that culture plays in creating the team you want, but you just need some help with a strategy and figuring out what to do next. Read this book to help yourself lead more intentionally.
3. **You're a seasoned people leader.** You've been around a while. This isn't your first rodeo when it comes to leading people, but right now you're not leading the team you want. Maybe the

culture you have isn't the culture you created or even the culture you want. Perhaps all the ingredients are there but you know they need to be refined and clarified, or simply harnessed and amplified. Read this book to help yourself accelerate the process.

What do we call you?

The term 'middle manager' has been around for decades as a label. But although it's an accurate description, I can't remember the last time I met somebody who introduced themselves as one. During the interview process, we asked people about their role and the title they most resonated with. Do people prefer to be called 'the middle manager', 'team leader', 'people leader' or just plain 'manager'?

The responses varied across the group. Those who preferred a title with the word 'manager' in it felt that their role encompassed more than just leading people. They felt they were managing processes as well as people and therefore found 'manager' to be more appropriate. Some also felt that 'manager' sounded more senior than 'team leader'. Those who preferred a title with the word 'leader' in it resonated more with the concept of leading their people by setting an example, rather than managing their people, which for some created connotations of 'micromanaging'. Some also felt the word 'manager' was outdated.

One thing was for sure: no one we spoke to resonated with the term 'middle manager', despite feeling like it most accurately described their position in the organisation.

After some long deliberation, we erased 'middle manager' from our vocabulary and landed on the term 'people leader'. Those we interviewed felt this best described the part of their role which is the largely the emphasis of this book – *leading people*. This was also the reasoning by which we excluded managers from the study who were not currently leading people in their role.

To clarify, using the title of 'people leader' in this book in no way negates the very important managerial functions of the role, and excluding managers from the study who were not currently leading a team of people in no way makes each of them less of a leader within their organisations.

Using this book

I'm not for a moment suggesting that this will be (or should be) the last book you read on culture, or that applying the concepts in this book will enable you to tick culture off your to-do list. This book is designed to help you with the structure you need to start a meaningful, intentional and ongoing conversation about the culture in your team.

What you'll find in this book is an important and helpful part of the picture of culture, but it would be arrogant for me to suggest that it is the complete picture. Academics, sociologists, anthropologists and business leaders alike have been trying to make sense of this complex thing called 'culture' for decades, and yet each time we peel back a layer we begin to discover more of its richness, complexity and diversity. What this book will do is begin to refine your palate to the conversation around culture. It will give you and your team a common language that dives deeper than simply 'good' or 'bad' in the culture conversation, so you can start creating the team you want. You can think about this book as your left-right combo of process (to help sharpen your thinking) and practical tools (to shape your working). But while I can help you with the framework, the decision to take action rests solely with you.

What we will talk about

This book is built around five conversations that you can have with your team. The first three conversations help you design the team culture you want. The final two help shape it. To set up these conversations, we need to have a conversation about culture. To wrap up these conversations, we need to know where to start and what to avoid. I've broken the book up into three parts:

1. **A conversation about culture:** let's talk about what culture is, why it matters and what you can do to get your team ready to talk about it.
2. **Culture conversations:** let's talk about the conversations you'll need to help you and your team design your culture more intentionally.
3. **Keeping the conversation going:** let's talk about what you'll need to bring your culture to life – where to start, what to avoid and how to shape it day to day.

Each chapter contains practical tips for applying your insights and ends with a short summary of the key points. You can use the conversations from this book to facilitate your next team day or space out the conversations over a period of time. You don't have to do it all right now: you just need to start where you are, with what you have.

When you're ready, let's talk about culture.

PART ONE

A CONVERSATION ABOUT CULTURE

Culture is your team's unseen competitive advantage. It sets winning teams apart. And yet, according to Google Trends, the top three most common searches associated with the topic of 'organisational culture' since 2004 have been:

- 'What is organisational culture'
- 'What is culture'
- 'Organisational culture definition'.

Despite all the information we have access to – and there is a lot – we're obviously all still a little confused about culture. So, before you can have conversations with your team about the culture you want, we need to talk about what culture is and what it's for. We need to make sense of why culture is so important and understand why it can feel a little confusing or even overwhelming. And then, as when building anything significant, we need to start by laying the foundations.

Chapter 1

We're all a little different

Celebrate your uniqueness

'There are two types of people. The first are people who think there are two types of people. The second are those who've accepted that everyone is tragically, and gloriously, different.'
– Karl Kristian Flores, *The Goodbye Song*

Key finding: Half of people leaders see inclusion and belonging as key ingredients of a healthy culture.

'You've got a look in your eye like you're about to do something crazy.'

I can remember this moment vividly. I was seated across the table from my first mentor, Lincoln, just inside the entrance of a small Italian restaurant. It wasn't the calming ambience or authentic pasta menu that left a strong impression on me (it had neither). Truth be told, we were only there because it was one of the few places that would stay open outside of the peak lunch rush in the small town I grew up in.

What made this moment so memorable was what I said out loud for the first time: 'I'm going to ask Cassandra to marry me.'

That might not sound like a profound decision to you, but it's not a decision a lot of 19-year-olds make. If you find yourself thinking 'You were just a kid', then that's a perfectly appropriate response. Don't get me wrong, Cassandra and I are both extremely grateful for the opportunity we have had to grow up together and experience so much life in common, but to this day we're still unsure why nobody tried to stop us.

Fast-forward six months, throw in a birthday, a wedding and a mortgage, and there we were – standing in the lounge room of our first home, living together for the first time away from our childhood homes, deciding what to eat for our first meal. As we began making our brand-new house a home, the realisation finally started to sink in: we were two very different and very complex human beings who now needed to live, work and function together in very close proximity with some semblance of harmony. All. The. Time.

We're all a little *different*. We all have those *things* – those things we do *differently* to everybody else. Those things that make perfect sense to us but make no sense at all when it comes time to share them with others. They could be nicknames, beliefs, phrases or ways of doing something. I invited people to share some of theirs with me in preparation for this book:

- Sarah told me how her mind was blown when she learned we say 'Bless you' after a sneeze and not 'Blashu'.
- Rose refers to paying by EFTPOS as 'booping' the card, and her children now believe that in order to pay, you must 'boop it'.
- Ed learned that adding the words 'so it is' at the end of a sentence might be normal in Northern Ireland – for example, 'It's a really nice day, so it is' – but that it didn't translate when he moved to Australia.

- The "'slow poach" or "slow coach"' conversation can really stir up some heated debate in Jesse and Chanelle's marriage. I didn't dare throw 'slowpoke' into the mix.
- Letitia's family uses the question 'How long shall we beep it for?' to refer to the microwave, and she wasn't made aware that this was unusual until getting married.
- Kat's family celebrates each Christmas present exchange with 'warm-up gifts' before exchanging the 'main' presents, so expect a very average first present if you attend Christmas at her house.

The list goes on. People told me about vacuum cleaners named Johnny, dog biscuits called 'hominigritz' and pet chickens called 'lah-lahs', all of which made perfect sense to them – and yet it was impossible to understand the origins of these terms.

My favourite story was from a participant who will remain name-less, who confidently asked if anybody in the group was ever given the 'scratchy towel' as a comforter when sick. (Her parents had a dedicated towel for when she was sick in case she threw up on it. Of course, they would ensure that towel was the oldest and most disposable towel in the cupboard, aka the 'scratchy' towel.) It was sad to see her happy childhood memory pulled out from underneath her.

The moment my wife walked in on me laying bath towels down at the doorways to our new home was when we discovered my 'different'. Let me explain.

I blame my stepfather's 'different' for influencing mine. He had an ability to maximise the life of absolutely everything we owned. This applied to everything from appliances to books, right down to the carpet in our house. In his defence, our home was immaculate and we rarely had to replace or fix anything. As a teenager, all of my friends would throw parties when their parents left them at home alone for the weekend; I was more excited about being able to eat in the lounge room on the carpet (with a blanket down, of course).

Bundaberg is a small town located in regional Queensland, Australia, known around the world for its rum, ginger beer and sugar. Growing up, we were told it was located on the same latitude as Hawaii, giving it the seventh-best climate in the world. (The more accurate description of 'hot and humid' is much less appealing for most tourism campaigns.) After a long day in the heat and humidity, you can imagine the condition in which my brother and I would arrive home when we were teenagers. While many households have a 'no shoes in the house' policy, ours went a little further: when we arrived home, we went straight to the outdoor tap, where a little bar of soap sat, to wash our feet and *prepare* to enter the house. There was no way we were going to be allowed to bring all that sweat and oil from our feet into the house across the pristine carpet. Naturally, once you'd entered the house, you'd need a towel to dry your feet before coming inside. My whole life, the towel at the door made perfect sense.

So, there I was, a newly married man setting up our freshly built home, when I see my wife just walk inside *without* washing her feet, like it was nothing, without a single hesitation, like some kind of animal. Then there was my wife, staring through the lounge-room window at me, in the backyard, with a bar of soap in one hand and the hose in the other like some kind of psychopath.

Don't be too quick to judge the differences. You have them, I have them, we all have them – we just think they're *normal*. We usually don't know they're unique, unusual or flat-out weird until we find someone else that does it *differently* to us. And where else can you see this play out better than at work?

'Different' shows up at work

I'm never surprised when I talk to people leaders and hear that there is conflict at work. I'm more concerned when they claim there isn't.

That more than likely points to a lack of diversity or a suppression of conflict. We spend more than a third of our lives at work, so it's bound to be one of the first places we start to notice that the way 'I' do things and the way 'you' do things can be extremely dissimilar. The workplace is a collision of differences.

Similarities might make us comfortable. But our differences make us better.

It's OK to have your differences. In fact, we need them and are better for them. We're not trying to create some beige, homogeneous blob in an organisation where we all think, walk, talk and act the same. We can leverage our differences to help us bring fresh perspectives and approaches to the way we work. We can contribute our uniqueness in order to spark new creative ideas and groundbreaking innovation.

In a 2009 study, fraternity and sorority students were placed in small groups to solve a murder mystery case and then asked to provide a joint answer. Five minutes in, they were joined by an additional member – either a person from their own house or an 'outsider'. Afterwards, they were asked to rate the conversation and process. When an outsider was added, students rated the conversation as less comfortable and less effective – and yet, their chance of arriving at the correct solution doubled (from 29 per cent to 60 per cent). While the work might have felt harder, the outcomes were actually better.

We might find it easier to be around people who are like us, but we get better when we surround ourselves with those who are anything but.

Frans Johansson is the author of the bestselling book *The Medici Effect*, which explores the vital role diversity plays in creativity. In the book, he explains that our most breakthrough creativity occurs at the intersection of different fields, ideas, people and cultures. In an interview on my podcast *Phone Calls With Clever People*, Frans shared a powerful example of how this diversity drives innovation.

In the mid-1990s in London, England, Great Ormond Street Hospital (GOSH) was experiencing an increase in complications between the operating room and the intensive care unit, which they attributed to the high risk involved in the handover procedure. When the hospital sought to improve its systems, you might naturally assume that they would identify other hospitals within the medical field to learn more about best practice and procedures. However, instead they chose to engage the Formula 1 pit crew at Ferrari.

A team of doctors visited and observed the pit crew handoff in Italy, taking particular note of their process mapping and description and delegation of tasks. In Formula 1 racing, the pit crew are able to complete the complex task of a tyre change and refuel in around seven seconds. The doctors at GOSH found this similar to the team effort of surgeons, anaesthetists and ICU staff who needed to transfer a patient, their equipment and information from the operating room to the ICU ward.

Following the trip to Italy, the team took time to videotape their handover procedures and sent the tapes to be reviewed by the team at Ferrari. This analysis of the procedure resulted in a new handover protocol with new and improved processes and more streamlined teamwork, which reduced complications at the hospital. For the hospital staff, a unique perspective transformed their patient care and increased safety. What value could a diverse perspective bring to your team?

Differences are advantages – a conversation with Corrie

I first met Corrie when we were speaking together at a retail conference in Melbourne back in 2019. We were seated at a table together, and from the moment I spotted her walking over, I knew there was something different about her. It wasn't her bright red lipstick, leopard-skin clothing or full-sleeve tattoos that made her stand out in a crowd in business attire: there was something unique about the way she carried herself and the confidence she had to show up and be true to who she was.

Corrie is the CEO of Thendro, the parent company of the retail store Off Ya Tree, which is well known across Australia. Founded in the 1970s by Jim Kouts as a small stall at the Queen Victoria Market in Melbourne, Thendro has grown to have more than 20 retail stores Australia-wide and is a wholesaler to businesses all over the country, with a revenue of over $30 million a year. Thendro has become one of the leading businesses in the areas of smoking paraphernalia and alternative fashion, and now operates the world's largest body piercing brand. The business prides itself on doing things in an unconventional way, thinking differently and being different. While the alternative products they provide serve a very specific market, it is what Corrie has done to shape the culture of the business that first caught my attention.

Corrie is the very definition of 'started from the bottom, now we're here'. Corrie began working at Thendro on the retail floor back in the late 1990s and rose through the ranks to lead the business as CEO. She shared with me what it was that attracted her to the business in the early days:

'I just loved alternative culture, tattooing, piercing, that kind of thing. It, to be fair, probably disgusted my parents somewhat. No one wanted to hire me: I had pink hair 20 years ago and I had a few tattoos. I was totally capable as a human being, but I wanted the right to look how I wanted to look. And so, it shut a lot of doors. It's nowhere near that anymore. I mean, you can go to a coffee shop and people have nose rings. And I remember, when I used to work in hospitality, you weren't allowed a nose ring. It was just all these rules and regulations.'

Many of the people who work at Thendro have endured a life of being ostracised by the external world, which is one of the complications of being someone who is into an alternative culture – whether it is being judged by family members or more mainstream people, or experiencing the looks you get while simply walking to work from the train station. Corrie and the team have worked hard to create an environment that welcomes and celebrates each person's differences:

'Our mantra is "helping anybody". Not everybody: anybody. And the emphasis is on the "any", because you can be anybody you want to be. If you say everybody, for me, that's meaning everyone's the same. So, we're very strong in that wording, but it's helping anybody to be who they truly are. And that's at a staffing level and a customer level. We want them to feel safe, secure and happy to be their real selves.

'So, we always welcome with open arms people that aren't welcomed by others. And so, I think you get a loyalty. There's a natural loyalty that [says], "Holy shit. You've seen me as a human being and you're okay with that? And you are still wanting to employ me and help build my career and my future?" And we're always about that, whether you're with us for a long time, or whether it's us giving you tools to further your career elsewhere: that's really important to us either way.

'We are getting the wrong-side-of-the-track people. And I don't necessarily mean just by the way people look: it's like their outlook on life, or that they want to just work three days a week and they don't necessarily have a career and that's comfortable, because to them, their hobbies are way more important. We're open to that and we're open to the flexibility of that.'

Corrie regularly points back to the organisation's mission with the hashtag #ThinkDifferentBeDifferent and told me that they are on a mission to be 'the best at being different'. During the COVID-19 pandemic, while many retail businesses were struggling, Corrie and the team at Thendro were able to maintain the strength of the business and not go backwards in most part due to their commitment to being different:

'Go back two years ago, the banks would say "You've got too many hands in too many pies, and who are you? You do body modification, you do smoking subculture stuff, you do alternative fashion?" and the banks couldn't get their head around it. They're like, "A shoe shop sells shoes, so they're an expert in shoes. You've got 16 different departments. How can you be an expert in all 16 of those departments?" Now, they're like, "Oh, the diverse companies are the ones that have survived the pandemic, and the ones that just sell shoes are the ones that have suffered".

'We do get told a lot what we should be doing, and we don't really listen, and I think it's been really positive. By us being unconventional and viewing the world differently, it's allowed us to pivot whenever we've needed to pivot, because different markets for us have always been down or up, [for example] you've had a slump in body piercing, and then your smoking goes up, and then your fashion goes through the roof. Because we have all the different departments, they all complement each other. And so, we have constant growth, which is really positive.'

Thendro is a business that doesn't just talk about acceptance, belonging and thinking differently. These principles are at the essence of their culture. They are lived out by their people from the bottom to the top of the organisation and set them apart as a workplace like no other:

> 'We just don't care how they present themselves, as long as they're doing what's required, but they're supporting everyone else in the team and the team is supportive of them.'

Thendro is proof that you don't need uniformity for alignment. They have built their organisation on the premise that difference is their advantage. We're not seeking to eradicate differences at work – we need them. But we also need them to work at work.

Different has to work at work

There's a question I love to ask the teams I work with to highlight just one aspect of this. Take a moment to consider how you would answer:

If you were delegated a big and complex project to work on, what would be the first thing you'd do to get started?

Would you think people's approach would mostly be the same? Here's just a small collection of answers I've been given over the years:

- 'The first thing I would do is ask a whole lot of questions to the person that delegated this to me so I can better understand the assignment.'
- 'I would want to know why this project is important to take on right now.'
- 'I'd be curious about how this connects to the overall strategic plan.'
- 'Get away from people. I need some space to think about it more strategically and get a plan in place. Only once I'm clear can I get other people involved.'

- 'I'd immediately gather a team of people to talk through the project and work out who would be best suited to help with different parts.'
- 'I think I would break it down into a series of smaller projects and then delegate appropriately.'

Did your answer show up in the list? Or would you do it differently? If I were to ask you which approach was *right*, which would you say? Generally speaking, they all are. We might be assigned the same task but all approach it differently. You could create an almost endless list of work-related functions this applies to.

Most of our career is spent thinking, working and operating at an individual level. When we join an organisation, we consider our place through the lens of 'me'. How will 'I' do things here? How do I fit in this team? How do the consequences of my behaviour impact me? How does my performance in this team influence my opportunities for promotion or limit my opportunities for advancement?

While differences are advantages, what happens when the way you or I do things gets in the way of our collective progress?

As leaders, we have a responsibility to the collective. This means considering how 'we' now do things as a team. How do 'we' communicate as a team? How do 'we' engage as a team? How do 'we' confront behaviours or manage conflict as a team? What and how do 'we' celebrate here?

This is a sobering new reality. It's no longer just about you. You are responsible for leading your team in a way that helps remove the ambiguity and finds a way for you to move forward together. You play a crucial role in helping people feel included and creating a shared sense of belonging.

Communication is the problem, communication is the solution

My journey can best be described as a long collision of marketing, leadership and psychology. I have always found myself in positions and organisations that straddle the intersection between business and people. This has taken me from my own consulting business to education, government, events and the not-for-profit sector. Wherever I go, the problems to manage always have one thing in common: communication.

If we can learn to have more effective conversations, we can almost always resolve our biggest issues. If we avoid them or leave communication open to interpretation or ambiguity, then they almost always escalate unnecessarily.

It's communication that has saved my marriage times over and communication that can transform a team. When I walked inside, having dried my feet on the fresh towel at the door, my wife lovingly looked at me and said, 'We need to talk'. As two very different people who had always approached life in a very *individual* way, we needed to have a conversation about how we would now live and function *together*.

An intentional culture is what is needed to make differences work at work.

I want to suggest to you that culture is the key to moving from individual to collective. It's how we align people so we can move forward together, and it's how we make our differences work at work. In Corrie's words, 'Yeah. Culture's it, mate'. And what you need to create the culture you want is more effective team conversations.

But first, let's talk about why culture is so important.

Action steps

Remember this

- We all do things that are a little different.
- Differences show up at work.
- Differences are advantages.
- Intentional culture is the key to making differences work at work. It's how we move from individual to collective.

Try this

Have a conversation with your team about the things that make them unique. Take time to explore the different perspectives. Here are some questions you could ask:

- What is something you do differently to anybody else?
- What is something that seems normal to you that other people might find unusual?
- What makes no sense to you when you see someone else doing it?
- What is something you're passionate about that is completely unrelated to your job?

Find ways to regularly appreciate and celebrate the unique perspectives of your team.

Work towards this

- Everyone in your team is aware of their uniqueness.
- Each team member recognises and appreciates the strength of diversity.

Chapter 2

The unseen advantage

Get clear on your purpose

'Culture is the invisible glue that holds an organisation together... [It] can act as a conduit for change, enhanced competitiveness and innovation, but it also can act as a serious obstacle to progress. Either way, managers ignore the influence of culture at their peril.' – Abby Ghobadian and Nicholas O'Regan

---

Key finding: Almost all people leaders (99%) believe that culture plays an integral role in the overall success of an organisation.

Culture is your unseen competitive advantage.

Imagine leading a team so well respected that new positions are inundated with applications from the market's top talent, or leading a team so engaged that your best people never want to leave. Think about what could be achieved if your team could collaborate better, make decisions more easily and adapt or respond to change faster. What would it mean to you and those you lead to show up each day to an environment that allows each person to be fully seen, heard and valued? How would you like your team to be known for its creativity, innovation and results that deliver tangible value to the business and impact your organisation's bottom line?

It's aspirational but entirely achievable. Culture is the key.

Almost all of the people leaders in our research (99 per cent) told us they believed that culture 'definitely' or 'somewhat' played an integral role in the overall success of an organisation, with a large proportion (74 per cent) of those responding with 'yes definitely'. While culture in many ways is an abstract or intangible concept, the results it delivers to you – the leader – your team and the organisation are very real and observable. Much like water to the goldfish, just because you are immersed in it doesn't mean the impact can't be felt in both subtle and significant ways.

With very little argument among leaders about the link between strong culture and organisational success, forgive me if it feels like I'm preaching to the choir. It's important to hold up the benefits clearly in front of you so that you'll know why culture is worth all the effort (and it is effort) you're going to invest.

The impact of culture

In our research we asked leaders where they believe culture has the largest impact on organisational success. Here's what we learned.

Culture can build a team that everybody wants to join

Eighty per cent of people leaders believe that culture has a massive or substantial impact on employee attraction and retention.

Gallup is a research company that has been studying organisations and teams across the world for more than 80 years. With data collected from over a million teams globally, they've learned a thing or two about organisational performance. Drawing on this research, the article 'Culture Wins by Attracting the Top 20% of Candidates' by Nate Dvorak and Ryan Pendell point out two compelling reasons why culture is your best attraction strategy.

The first is that strong culture is how we create 'employees that become brand advocates', with 71 per cent of employees saying that the way they learn about job opportunities is a referral from current employees of an organisation. Your team culture may not have a LinkedIn profile, it's not at barbecues on the weekend talking with prospective employees and it doesn't speak at conferences about how great it is to work in your team – but your people are, and they are talking about your culture. It's why you should never underestimate the reach and influence of a raving fan or the damage that can come from a disgruntled employee.

Their second insight is that talented people proactively seek out organisations with exceptional culture. That is, the top 20 per cent of talent are more likely to ask questions relating to your culture. Dvorak and Pendell found that the most talented candidates ask questions like 'Who will my manager be?', 'How will I learn and grow here?' and 'What does this company stand for?' In contrast, they found that less talented prospects will ask transactional questions relating to issues like pay, perks and hours.

When culture is strong, people have a unified, honest and convincing language to describe to prospective employees what it's like to work on your team. When culture is strong, it has a gravitational pull that attracts high calibre people into your orbit.

Culture can build a team that nobody wants to leave

Of all the areas people leaders believe culture has the greatest impact on, employee engagement is at the top of the list, with 83 per cent saying it has a massive or substantial impact.

With global engagement scores as low as 20 per cent, according to Gallup's study of 2.7 million employees, every leader needs a strategy to ensure they retain their best people. Not only is the investment of your time and money to train a new employee costly, you also lose valuable corporate knowledge when a person exits the business. While culture is not simply the results of your engagement score, this score will influence it. Culture can be difficult to quantify, but engagement data can tell a valuable story about what it's like to work in your team or organisation.

From a study of nearly 4000 skilled employees, the *Hays Salary Guide FY21/22* revealed the top reasons employees are looking for another job. Alongside a lack of promotional opportunities and a competitive salary, it was 'poor management and workplace culture' that made it into the top three for more than a third of respondents. Culture isn't just your best attraction strategy, it's also your most valuable retention strategy, because it's a driving factor in employee engagement. A Columbia University study showed that the likelihood of job turnover at an organisation where culture was strong sat at just 13.9 per cent, in contrast to organisations with weak company culture where turnover was as high as 48.4 per cent.

When culture is strong, you keep the right people, which goes a long way in moving the needle of engagement.

Culture can build a team that moves forward faster

Eighty per cent of people leaders believe that culture has a massive or substantial impact on the achievement of organisational goals.

Whether it's rapidly shifting organisational priorities or simply responding to the unforeseen challenges that derail our best-laid plans (such as a global pandemic), the only thing leaders can be certain about is change. When you're staring down the barrel of disruption, you need a team that can reduce the friction of decision-making in order to move quickly and flexibly. You want people who can collaborate just as effectively while dispersed and connecting through a computer screen as when seated across from each other in the boardroom. You need 'can-do' people who aren't thrown by the requirements of a new path forward.

In 2021, PwC released the findings of their global culture survey exploring the link between culture and competitive advantage, and they found that it's these three aspects of adaptability, collaboration and decision-making that set apart organisations with a distinctive culture. Of the people and organisations they surveyed, 81 per cent of respondents who strongly believed their organisation was able to adapt during the 12 months before the survey (during a global pandemic) also said their culture has been a source of competitive advantage. Seventy-three per cent of participants said that making decisions quickly became easier or stayed the same during the pandemic when there was a distinctive culture, compared with 57 per cent when there was not. Collaboration stayed the same or improved for 64 per cent of participants in organisations with a distinctive culture, in contrast to 49 per cent without a distinctive culture.

When culture is strong, you create an environment that enables people to adapt quicker, collaborate better and decide faster, which every team needs to do to accelerate progress and achieve goals.

Culture can build a team that is physically and psychologically safe

Eighty per cent of people leaders believe that culture has a massive or substantial impact on psychological safety and 73 per cent share that belief about physical safety.

In 1999, Amy Edmondson published her influential paper 'Psychological Safety and Learning Behavior in Work Teams', which became the catalyst for much discussion around the role of psychological safety in high performing teams. Her research into medical team errors between departments in the same hospital sought to understand whether the most cohesive teams made fewer errors. Surprisingly, she learned that the most cohesive teams actually reported making the most mistakes. What became apparent was that these cohesive teams were more able and willing to talk about their mistakes. In an interview with *HBR IdeaCast*, she explains why this kind of psychological safety is so rare:

> 'It is an instinct to want to look good in front of others. It's an instinct to divert blame, you know, it's an instinct to agree with the boss. And hierarchies are places where these instincts are even more exaggerated.'

Psychological safety enables the people on your team to show up fully at work without fear of humiliation or punishment. Your team's culture around failure, disagreement, feedback and recognition will determine the extent to which this is possible.

Psychological safety can determine whether a person brings their whole self to work. It means little if that person is not physically safe when they do. Physical safety can mean the difference between a person going home to those they love at the end of the day or not. Culture helps us determine what is acceptable here and what is not, and that plays a crucial role in reducing the number of decisions that could be harmful or fatal.

When culture is strong, you can create an environment that keeps people safe – in every sense of the word.

Culture can build a team that helps people to belong

Eighty per cent of the people leaders in our study told us that culture has a massive or substantial impact on inclusion and diversity.

Fiona Robertson is my good friend, a culture expert and a fellow Major Street author. Fiona was a guest on my podcast *Phone Calls With Clever People*, where we ask great questions of talented leaders to help people become more effective leaders. She shared her definition of culture, which is also the title of her brilliant book: *Rules of Belonging*. She likened these rules to the popular 1990s movie *The Matrix* in that, when you begin to see them at play at work, it will be near impossible to unsee them. She encourages us to ask, 'What does it take for people to belong on this team?' Through culture, we learn what is tolerated and what is not in our quest for human connection and belonging.

When culture is strong, it is clear what it takes to belong. We've already established that the goal of culture is not to eradicate difference. The focus isn't even on agreement: you don't need to agree with everything in the organisation to have alignment in your team. Culture is the strategy that enables us to make these differences work at work.

Culture can build a team that thinks differently

Seventy-eight per cent of people leaders believe that culture has a massive or substantial impact on creativity and innovation.

You might be familiar with TED Talks or may have even had the privilege of attending a local TEDx event, which take place all over the globe. In 2015, Head of TED Chris Anderson ran an experiment at TED's headquarters. Each staff member was given a day off per fortnight to study something. They called it 'Learning Wednesdays', and it was a chance for people to explore and learn something they were passionate about. As an organisation they had a culture of lifelong learning, and Chris believed this was practising what they preached. To avoid it becoming another day off in front of the TV, the condition was that everyone had to commit at some point in the year to delivering a TED Talk to the rest of the staff about what they had learned. As a result, the rest of the business was able to benefit from the learning.

When was the last time your people were given the time, resources and permission to play or learn? How does your team respond to failure or risk? Is it encouraged or punished? Would you describe your team as curious or judgmental when ideas are shared? The answers can reveal a lot about your team's culture and, in turn, tell an interesting story about your team's ability to innovate and be creative.

When the culture is strong, people know what freedom they have to create and innovate.

Culture can build a team that delivers results

Seventy-four per cent of people leaders believe that culture has a massive or substantial impact on revenue and profit.

While revenue and profit sit at the bottom of the list of areas impacted by culture, they are in no way less valuable. Put simply, strong culture shows up in the bottom line in business. The research from PwC mentioned earlier found that organisations that have a distinctive culture were 48 per cent more likely to have reported an increase in revenue during the global pandemic. Research from McKinsey of over 1000 organisations made up of more than three million individuals found that those with top quartile cultures posted a return to shareholders 60 per cent higher than median companies and 200 per cent higher than those in the bottom quartile.

In each of the areas we've discussed, there is not only an outcome benefit, such as innovation or inclusion, but each outcome has a financial implication. When the right employees connect with your culture, they're more likely to be engaged and less likely to leave, which has a financial consequence.

The right people don't stay in the wrong culture, and the right culture will quickly weed out the wrong people. When you can keep the right people, the top 20 per cent, Gallup says that organisations realise:

- 41 per cent less absenteeism
- 70 per cent fewer safety incidents
- 59 per cent less turnover
- 17 per cent higher productivity
- 21 per cent higher profitability.

Culture might be unseen, but its impact is certainly not.

The Great Re...evaluation

Few events have created such a catalytic sense of change globally as the COVID-19 pandemic. At the time of writing in 2022 we're still working out the long-term consequences of global disruption. After more than a year of uncertainty, over 3.9 million Americans resigned from their jobs in June 2021, a trend which was dubbed 'The Great Resignation' by Dr Anthony C. Klotz, an associate professor at Texas A&M University. In an interview with *The Washington Post*, Dr Klotz identified four primary reasons employees were opting for greater work-life balance, better compensation and more meaningful careers:

1. **Resignation backlog:** In the midst of uncertainty, those who may have typically resigned decided to stay, creating a backlog of people waiting to resign.
2. **Increased fatigue:** There were heightened levels of burnout across all layers of business, which is a predictor of resignation.
3. **Identity shift:** Pandemic epiphanies led people to make major shifts in their life.
4. **Working conditions:** After a year of working from home, many employees were not excited to return to the office and were choosing to leave organisations that did not support flexible working.

Throughout the global pandemic, restrictions and lockdowns forced people home to be with their thoughts. There are only so many loaves of banana bread or sourdough you can bake before you are left reflecting on what really matters.

Whether or not The Great Resignation is real or hype – and whether it will touch other parts of the globe – is a discussion still underway, with much heated debate. However, one thing is clear: the global pandemic has initiated a period of global re-evaluation. People are checked out emotionally, burned out physically, figuring themselves out mentally and opting out of things that don't align personally; and whatever you choose to call it, that reality is not going away quickly.

A pay cheque and perks might get people's attention, and a ping-pong table in the break room might make lunchtime more enjoyable, but the culture is your team's best unseen competitive advantage.

Action steps

Remember this

Culture is your unseen competitive advantage. When culture is strong:

- You attract and retain the best people.
- You adapt more quickly, collaborate better and decide faster, which helps you accelerate progress and achieve your goals.
- You create teams in which people feel safe to show up fully, knowing they will be protected from harm.
- You help people find a greater sense of belonging, share their perspectives with a greater degree of confidence and deliver results that shift the bottom line in business.

Try this

Take time to consider why culture is important to you and your team. You could ask the following questions:

- What areas that culture impacts would most benefit the team or organisation right now? Examples include engagement, retention, collaboration, adaptability, decision-making, safety, belonging, creativity and results.
- What are some of the ways our current culture creates a competitive advantage?

Work towards this

- You and your team see the value of working towards an intentional culture.
- You have a clear purpose and personal commitment to creating a culture by design.
- You can clearly demonstrate to your manager the value of investing in culture.

Chapter 3

The problem with culture

Remove your roadblocks

'If you want to provoke a vigorous debate, start a conversation on organizational culture.' – Michael D. Watkins

---

Key finding: Half of people leaders believe that culture cannot be influenced – it just happens.

When I first approached McCrindle to discuss the possibility of us working together on a research project that would help us understand what people leaders experience and believe about culture, I had already formed a few hypotheses about what we might discover. In large part those hypotheses proved to be accurate – with one exception.

With so many resources and tools aimed at organisational leaders and executive leaders, I questioned whether people leaders would see culture as a relevant part of their role. Were they thinking about it as much as the senior leaders of the organisation? With so much day-to-day responsibility in managing people, was it even registering on the list of priorities? Or, more importantly, did they even care?

The answer to that was a resounding 'yes'.

More than four in five people leaders believed that creating a healthy culture is a crucial element of their role, with 84 per cent of the leaders we asked telling us that creating a healthy culture was either 'the most' or 'one of the most' important parts of their role. Just 14 per cent of the remaining people leaders told us it was 'at least as important' as other aspects of their role, and fewer than 2 per cent said it was 'the least' or 'one of the least' important parts of their role.

Does culture matter? Absolutely. But as we dig a little deeper, we start to reveal some of the bigger problems with culture that people leaders have in common. I've grouped the problems into three dilemmas:

1. The definition dilemma – what is culture?
2. The leadership dilemma – who is responsible for culture?
3. The skills dilemma – how do you build culture?

The definition dilemma – what is culture?

Culture is easy to describe but hard to define.

While we all seem to agree that culture is a crucial part of leading a team, we still struggle to define exactly what culture is. Instead, most people we asked leaned towards describing the outcomes of culture. When we surveyed people leaders, we asked two questions to help us to understand this:

1. Do you have a clear understanding of what culture is?
2. How would you define team or organisational culture?

If you can get away with pretending you know in the first question, you certainly won't be able to get away with it in the second question. In response to the first question, we were surprised to learn just how confident people felt in being able to define it. Two thirds of people leaders believed they 'definitely' had an understanding of what culture is, with just 2.1 per cent of people leaders acknowledging they didn't really know.

The definition dilemma came to life with question two. When we asked people leaders a question that required them to write their definition of culture, only a little over one in ten were able to give us a definition that was in some way consistent with an academic or broader understanding of culture.

Many, rather than describing what culture is, described the evidence of what they believed to be healthy culture using words such as 'positive', 'inclusive' and 'valuing of individuals'. Some people defined culture in the following ways:

- 'We are inclusive and supportive; we work together to get the job done.'
- 'Collaboration and teamwork.'
- 'I would describe it as really organised.'

And, of course, one of my favourites and a surprisingly popular response:

- 'Good.'

When we dived deeper in conversation with a small selection of people leaders for our qualitative research and gave them time to consider their responses, we were able to get a little closer to some kind of meaningful definition. Here are two of the responses we received:

- 'Culture is the way that the embedded beliefs and values of an organisation are lived out. The way things are. They are those unquestioned ways of working that appear to be unintentional, but they are probably the result of lots of decisions made over many years.'

- 'Culture is that alignment towards a single mission or single set of values. It's buy-in, on an individual basis, to whatever the mission of the organisation is. It's individual commitment outside of "I'm getting paid to do this job".'

And yet, some responses still reverted to describing what healthy culture looks like:

'Culture is a sense of belonging, feeling part of a team… It's feeling proud about the things you do, like you're a part of something bigger. You've got each other's back and you buy into what the business believes in.'

We think we should know, but here is where the results take an interesting turn. The most consistent definition from participants was this:

'Organisational culture is the collection of values, expectations, and practices that guide and inform the actions of all team members.'

As I scanned through the results, I found that slight variations and adaptations of this definition consistently showed up. Perhaps there was an addition or subtraction of a few words, or a variation of the same idea, but in most part it was the same definition. Was it a coincidence that these people could articulate this definition near perfectly? Unlikely. I put myself in their position and considered what I would do if I didn't know the answer to something. I would turn to the source of all knowledge and wisdom: Google.

I opened a new tab and searched, "What is organisational culture?" And I'm confident you won't be surprised at what showed up as the top response:

'Organisational culture is the collection of values, expectations, and practices that guide and inform the actions of all team members.'

This definition comes from a popular online article titled 'Organizational Culture: Definition, Importance, and Development' published by an online employee experience platform. Not only did most of the people in our study struggle to define culture, a large portion of those who did found their answer online.

Are people embarrassed to admit they don't know what culture is? Is there an unspoken pressure to be able to explain this concept because we all know it is a vital part of our role? I wouldn't find that hard to believe. 'Culture' is a term we throw around liberally at work, and we hear those in senior leadership positions talking about it incessantly, but when it comes to making sense of it, we seem to all struggle to get on the same page.

You're not alone. Before you're tempted to beat yourself up, this confusion isn't reserved for people leaders. In 2012, a Deloitte culture survey found that while 94 per cent of executives and 88 per cent of employees know culture is important to business success, less than a third report they really understand their culture. In almost all of the interviews I conducted with senior leaders and organisational leaders in preparation for this book, I asked the same question: 'How would you define organisational or team culture?'

The responses were varied, from broad ideas such as 'the way we do things around here' to very specific definitions of the observable elements of culture such as 'behaviours' and 'systems'.

Some people like to use metaphors in an attempt to explain culture. They talk about culture as your 'team glue' or 'business operating system'. Others say culture is the 'wind' that propels you. For some, it's your 'organisational soil' and for others it's like an 'organisation's personality'. Again, these metaphors tend to describe what culture is *like* as opposed to what culture *is*.

The one thing that has become clear about culture is that culture is *not* clear.

Why is culture so hard to define?

Culture is so challenging to define because right now a *universal* understanding of culture just doesn't exist. As each person seeks to better understand culture through their own perspective, we see more of its complexity and a new definition emerges. It reminds me of our understanding of space: the further we explore, the more we learn about its vastness. It's important to say that the existing definitions are not wrong. They all show a unique perspective. We're all looking at the same painting, but we're all pointing at different parts.

In a 1998 article, Willem Verbeke, Marco Volgering and Marco Hessels identified 54 different definitions of the concept of organisational culture in articles and books between 1960 and 1993. These definitions preceded the launch of many of our popular online information-sharing platforms, so you can imagine how many more definitions there must be today.

What we do know is that, while a universal understanding of culture does not necessarily exist, there are some common themes. In the 54 definitions, Verbeke, Volgering and Hessels were able to identify some common language that appeared across all of the definitions, shown in Table 1.

Table 1: Organisational culture (54 definitions)

Rank	Language	Frequency
1	Members	40
1	Shared	40
3	Values	30
4	Organisation	28
5	Behaviour	27
6	Beliefs	23

Rank	Language	Frequency
7	Patterns	21
8	Norms	17
9	Learned	16
10	Way	15
10	Meanings	15
12	System	12
13	Assumptions	11
14	Social	10
15	Set	9
16	Practices	8
17	Understandings	7

If we take a step back and look at what connects these words, we can identify four key elements of culture that can help us better make sense of what it's all about:

1. **There is a collective element:** Culture is a shared experience. The use of words like 'shared', 'norms', 'members', 'organisation' and 'assumptions' points to the idea that culture is collective, not individual, and that it is through culture that we are able to arrive at some sense of group identity. Because culture is collective, it is able to endure when some people arrive or leave.

2. **There is an unseen element:** Culture has an intangible influence. When people seek to define culture, they include elements which are hard to measure and typically unseen, such as 'values', 'beliefs', 'understandings' and 'meanings'. While they may not be possible to measure, they are an underlying set of factors that guide expectations and influence culture.

3. **There is an observable element:** Culture has an observable impact. While culture is partly influenced by an unseen set of factors, there is no doubt that elements of culture are observable in nature. We can see this in 'behaviour', 'system', 'practices', 'patterns' and 'way' (of doing things). It shows up in the way we act, respond and communicate.

4. **There is a social learning element:** Culture is learned and dynamic. We are observing the responses of those around us *socially* to better understand how to interpret culture.

We owe much to early culture pioneers such as Edgar H. Schien, Larry Senn, Robert Cooke, John Kotter, James Heskett and many others who have brought these elements to light over the years in their own unique ways. You can see these elements embedded into some of the earliest definitions of culture from these great minds.

Schien wrote that culture is 'a pattern or system of beliefs, values, and behavioral norms that come to be taken for granted as basic assumptions and eventually drop out of awareness'. Kotter and Heskett wrote that it refers to 'values that are shared by the people in a group and that tend to persist over time even when group membership changes. At the more visible level, culture represents the behaviour patterns or style of an organisation that new employees are automatically encouraged to follow by their fellow employees'.

Our biggest threat, though, is that we spend more time defining culture than we do applying it. The problem with heading down the rabbit hole of academia and literature is that it is seemingly never-ending. And this information overwhelm seems to have created a great deal of confusion for leaders.

'What is the right definition of culture?' is the wrong question. The more helpful question is, 'What do I need to know in order to take action on culture?'

It's one thing to describe it, another to define it. But what ultimately matters is that we know how to apply it. Is culture 'the way we do things around here'? Yes. Is it much more than that? The answer is also yes.

What can we learn from the wisdom of many great culture pioneers, and what do you need in order to apply the insights from this book? You need to know that your team is consistently learning from what they observe around them. They are using that information to make sense of and interpret what the unspoken set of expectations is that enables them to belong or function according to what is normal in your team. These norms determine what is accepted or rejected, encouraged or discouraged, within the group. Over time they can even become so deeply ingrained that people become completely unaware of their existence.

The leadership dilemma – who is responsible for culture?

The priority is clear, but the responsibility is confusing.

When it comes to culture as a priority, people leaders agree that it's one of the most important parts of their role, if not the most important. However, what this responsibility entails looks different to different people. Some leaders believe their key responsibility is to set an example for their team by purely living out the culture they want to see. Other leaders recognise that this isn't just the responsibility of leaders alone but needs to be a shared responsibility of all employees throughout the organisation. Many leaders are intentional about modelling behaviours that reflect the organisational values and mission, while others are simply trying to model what they believe are good behaviours.

One of the leaders we interviewed explained their responsibility as 'being a nice human', suggesting to us that culture is often overcomplicated:

'I believe my key responsibility in shaping culture is to be a nice human. I think we overthink this, personally. I appreciate there's a lot of different strands to it in terms of the research. But it comes down to humanity for me. Possibly one of the driving forces of why we have such challenges with [culture] is because not everyone is a super nice human being sometimes. They've got polarising agendas or individual agendas, particular personality traits that don't really fit well with the role that they're in. "Square peg in a round hole" comes to mind and suddenly you've got yourself a toxic situation.'

Can culture be influenced? If so, who is responsible, and how much reach and influence can a people leader really have?

In our research we asked leaders to indicate the extent to which they agree with this statement about culture:

Culture is not something that can be influenced; it just happens.

The results were confronting and alarming.

Half of the people leaders in our study told us that they somewhat or strongly agree that culture is not something that can be influenced. That number seemed unusually high. We made the decision to go deeper in our qualitative interviews to understand what people really meant.

Culture may just happen, but good culture needs a strategy

When we asked people leaders how culture is built, 95 per cent of them told us that culture is a series of small decisions made over time.

This was one of the first clues that helped us understand what leaders believe about culture formation. If culture is built on the small, daily decisions that accumulate over time, then it's understandable that people would see culture-building as something that is seemingly unavoidable. We make decisions every day that shape a culture, even if it is not the culture we want. What emerged from our conversations is the distinction between a *culture by default* versus a *culture by design*. One participant described it as the unintentional consequence of doing what's right:

> 'Sometimes people can build really positive culture unintentionally by just going about doing what's right for their colleagues and customers. By default, they end up building a really good culture around them.'

Can culture be influenced? The answer is 'no' if you interpret that question to mean, 'Can you do anything to influence whether culture exists or not?' Each day, a leader and their team make decisions that shape the culture. But when it comes to building the culture you want, people leaders told us that is definitely something that can and should be influenced.

- 'Culture is almost always influenced. I think it definitely organically occurs off the back of a few key elements, like values and mission. I think if they're there and people are aligned to those, that influences culture enough that it is able to naturally occur but within the realms of some level of control.'
- 'Culture happens naturally but good culture can be intentionally built. When you draw attention to something, and you call it out and you have buy-in, then it's something that everyone owns. It's not just, "We think this is how we operate, and we talk about it". There's more authenticity to it because you're intentionally going after it.'

- 'Culture needs to be worked at strategically and regularly discussed with employees.'

You may not be able to influence whether culture exists, but you can influence what kind of culture exists. Great culture needs to be intentionally defined and followed up with strategy. They say that culture eats strategy for breakfast, but it might just be biting the hand that feeds it.

Who carries the responsibility of intentionality?

One participant said: 'We are all responsible [for creating good culture]. Culture happens everywhere. When you recognise you are a participant of that, you have a role to play in it. Not just managers, not just leaders'.

Everyone is responsible for culture, but in the words of John C. Maxwell, 'Everything rises and falls on leadership'.

We wanted to know who people leaders believe is responsible for the common aspects of culture formation. We identified five key areas and asked people leaders to select whether it was the head of the organisation, C-suite or executive leaders, managers or team leaders, the HR department, or employees who carry the responsibility. (They could select more than one option.) This is what we found:

1. **Setting the culture:** 75 per cent of people leaders believe that the head of the organisation is responsible for setting culture, while only 54 per cent of people leaders say it is their role.
2. **Leading the culture:** 65 per cent of people leaders believe that the C-suite or executive leadership team are responsible for leading the culture, while only 56 per cent of people leaders say it is their role.
3. **Communicating the culture:** 70 per cent of people leaders believe that they are responsible for communicating the culture, while only 51 per cent believe it is the role of the executive team.

4. **Living out the culture:** 58 per cent of people leaders believe they are responsible for living out the culture day to day, while only 51 per cent say it is the responsibility of the executive team.
5. **Addressing cultural inconsistencies:** 56 per cent of people leaders believe they are responsible for addressing the day-to-day cultural inconsistencies within their team, while only 49 per cent say it is the responsibility of the executive team.

Figure 1: Who is responsible for culture?

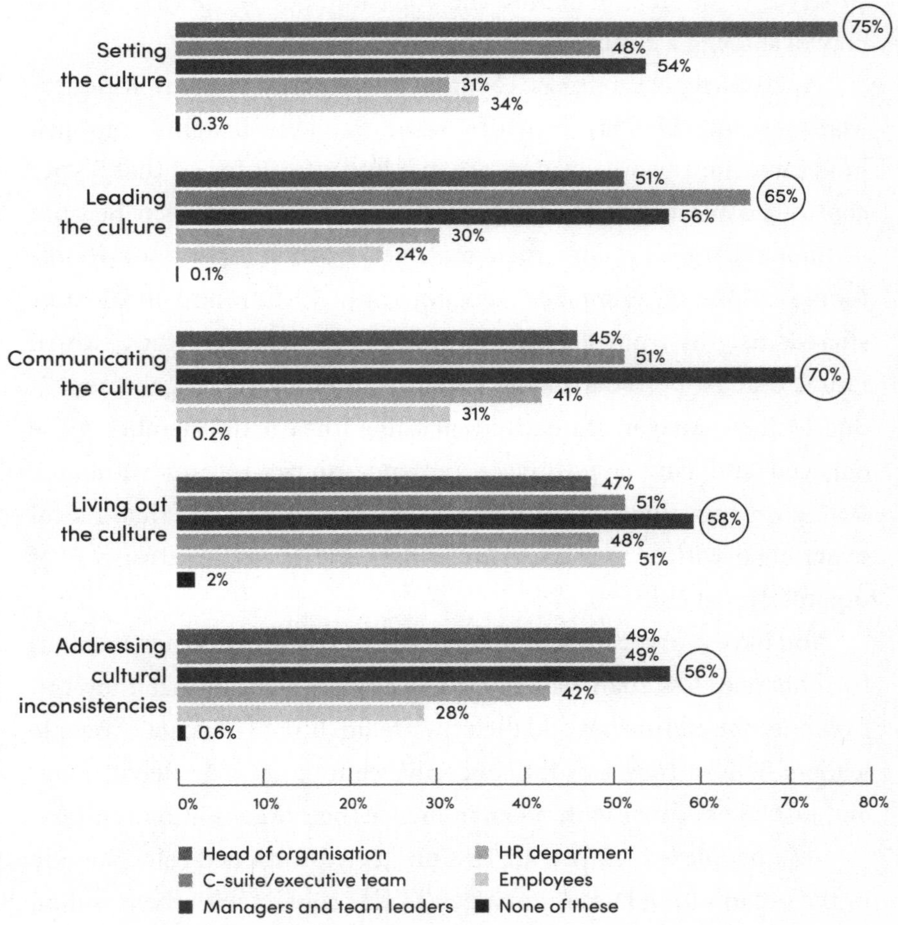

People leaders believe that while the top layers of the organisation are responsible for setting and leading the culture, they are ultimately the people who carry the weight of ensuring that this culture is lived out day to day.

The role of the people leader in culture cannot be understated. It's true that your CEO, board and managing director play important roles in defining the culture that helps align your organisation, and that your executive leadership team also carries the responsibility of ensuring they model the espoused culture of your business. But look closely at these areas of culture and you cannot deny the vital role you play in shaping a culture by design.

A 2021 report released by the Society for Human Resource Management (SHRM) provides some valuable insights into just how important people leaders are in a business. It found that 53 per cent of people who left an organisation due to culture left because of their relationship with their manager. In their 2019 book *It's the Manager: Moving from Boss to Coach*, Jim Clifton and Jim Harter shared insights from Gallup's largest global manager study, which found that 70 per cent of the variance in employee engagement is due to the manager. It's entirely possible for a team member to be engaged and have a positive experience on your team without a strong organisational culture; however, it's also possible that a local experience with a manager can undermine even the strongest of organisational cultures.

You have more reach and influence than you think. When it comes to influence, less than half of people leaders believe that they can influence the culture beyond their own team. Just 43 per cent of people leaders believe they can influence the culture of their department, and just 25 per cent say they can influence their organisation's culture.

As a people leader, you are in a uniquely positioned role. Nobody in the organisation has as much day-to-day contact with the frontline employees of your business than you. Your reach is substantial;

however, many people leaders I speak to tell me that they feel like the scope of their authority is limited. You're often leading decisions you did not make, which means you need to put out fires you did not start. You're most likely the first point of contact for staff problems and often receive the least amount of investment.

And if you are wondering whether or not your executive leaders see that, they do. In numerous interviews with executive and organisational leaders, they reiterated to me the invaluable role of their people leaders in shaping the organisation's culture. Jessica Sharpe is the Chief People Officer for Australia at Entain, one of the world's largest sports betting and gaming groups, and she captured the essence of what almost all of the other executive leaders told me:

> '...they are under so much pressure to lead and execute, more so than executives are at our level. And so I think they're one of the quickest groups to get tainted. And then if they do, their impact on the culture is so significant because they have such a broad reach...'

Nearly 80 per cent of the leaders in our study believe that they influence their own team (hilariously, this sits even higher than their ability to influence themselves, at 69 per cent), but for many leaders this is where the influence ends. It's a mindset that needs to shift. You may not have the authority to make all the decisions, but you do have the influence to shape how those decisions are enacted. You may not have the title that gives you a large platform, but you have the daily contact that gives you significant reach and impact in the business. When you influence your team, you multiply your reach and impact in the business. Don't believe the unhelpful story people often tell themselves, that you can't have reach or influence without title or authority.

Yes, everyone is responsible for culture, but culture needs a leader. You are that leader. Culture can be influenced, but it needs intentionality. You don't need to wait for someone else to start leading the culture – you can start right now, right where you are.

The skills dilemma – how do you build culture?

There's an abundance of training but an absence of confidence.

How often do you receive training on how to shape culture within your team? Eight out of ten people leaders in our study told us they received training at least once a quarter. This included people who said they received training either on an ongoing basis, monthly or quarterly. And yet just 3 per cent of people leaders said they feel completely confident to build great culture. Where is the disconnect? If we go back to the first dilemma, I believe we can gain some insight.

During our interviews, we asked people leaders about the training they received from their organisation, and the answers varied from one organisation to another. Some provide a multitude of professional development opportunities for people leaders, while others offer no formal training at all. But when the definition of culture is so broad, complex and even straight-up confusing at times, it's possible that people could see every training opportunity as an investment in culture. Courageous conversations training will shape your team's response to conflict, so you could say that it was training on how to shape culture. But that wasn't what we wanted to know. When we asked about formal training on how to shape the culture of their team, less than a quarter of people leaders we interviewed had received that kind of training. And when we asked people leaders in our quantitative survey what they needed to help them grow their ability to build great culture, over half of them told us they needed practical advice for how to shape culture within a team.

During our in-depth interviews, participants were asked to reflect on the key challenges they currently face with respect to culture and the areas in which they would like to grow. Leaders were most likely to present these challenges in the form of questions. We grouped these questions into four overall themes.

How much should you prioritise culture?

Leaders want to feel confident they are doing enough. Some people leaders find it challenging to know how much they should prioritise culture in their schedule. How much should they talk about culture with their team? And what is a good cadence for talking about culture with their team? Our research found that leaders most commonly invest three to four hours per month into shaping culture, with nine in ten leaders believing they should be investing more time.

How do you develop an effective strategy around culture?

Leaders want to feel confident they know what to do. People leaders working in an organisation without a strategy for culture wanted to understand how to develop an effective strategy and formalise values and cultural expectations within their team. How can they move from an informal, intuitive approach to an approach that has a particular direction and aligns with the goals of the organisation? One leader, who was working in an organisation experiencing rapid growth, asked, 'How do you know what changes you need to make now to achieve the culture you want in the future?' In Part Two of this book, we're going to walk through a practical strategy you can apply to shape the team culture you want.

How do you get people on board with culture?

Leaders want to feel confident their team is with them. By far the most challenging area for leaders is knowing how to motivate people when it comes to culture. These leaders are looking to understand how to connect with their team, how to create 'buy-in' to the culture and how to keep people motivated in the long term. They asked questions such as, 'How do you get people on board with the culture?', 'How do you model the culture you want to see?' and 'How can you tell if people are the right cultural fit when you are hiring?'

How do you measure cultural success?

Leaders want to know what it looks like to win. Some leaders are looking for guidance on how to measure whether someone is living out the organisational culture, given that it is subjective. Others are looking for ways to assess whether culture is changing in a healthy or an unhealthy way. In short, leaders are looking for tools to measure whether they are achieving their cultural strategy.

With so many big questions, where do you go to find the answers? Leaders told us that they mostly learn how to shape culture through observation, experience and mentoring. This style of 'training' is more ongoing than formal courses or workshops and, for many leaders, helps them to learn practical skills they can apply straight away in their context. Regular coaching or mentoring allows people to talk through their current challenges and receive guidance from someone with more experience:

'My manager is an awesome coach and really values culture. On an informal level I would receive coaching weekly around the challenges that we have in the team around shaping culture. We have to be really strategic at the moment because we are going through a lot of change, and we really want the end result to be a team that is well connected.'

But what do you do in the absence of experienced coaches or mentors? You could always learn through trial and error and figure it out, as shared by some of our participants:

- 'My training certainly hasn't been formal. To be honest, I think I've just gone in and tried things and made mistakes.'
- 'A lot of practice and realising over the years what doesn't work. Theory is really important to have some credibility. A heck of a lot of reading. I read a lot of books. Practice and age.'

When the directions are clear, the journey is calm

I'm not sure what the cultural norms are in your household, but in mine there are a certain set of expectations about the role of the passenger when driving to a destination. My role as the driver of the vehicle is in the name – my sole purpose is to operate the vehicle. My wife, as the passenger, has the very important function of ensuring our destination is entered correctly into the GPS so we can all feel confident in where we are going. After numerous performance reviews, it's a role she is still yet to cheerfully accept.

Of course, if you know where you're going it's possible to find your way there without the map – you'll just need to keep an eye out for the signs and be ready to course-correct when needed. But let's face it, life is so much simpler when you have some clear directions. You don't need to feel overwhelmed or anxious when you have a process to follow. When it comes to designing and shaping the culture you want, it's possible that you'll get there through some trial and error and some painful mistakes along the way.

Throughout the remainder of the book, I'm going to attempt to remove some of the guessing or interpretation by giving you some practical directions you can follow. We're going to explore the answers to some of these important, burning questions. In doing so, my goal is to remove some of the frustration or pain of avoidable mistakes and accelerate the journey towards your desired destination.

Culture may be hard to define, but what matters is that you have an understanding that you can apply. Culture may be everybody's responsibility, but it needs leadership, and that leader is you. At times culture may leave you with more questions than answers and more content than confidence, but with the right strategy and a commitment to the process, you can create the culture you want.

Action steps

Remember this

- While most leaders know that culture matters, that doesn't mean that culture is easy.
- The definition dilemma refers to culture being easy to describe but hard to define. While culture can be defined in an overwhelming number of ways, some common themes exist to help us make sense of it. Rather than being overwhelmed by what you don't know, focus on what you do. Instead of getting hung up on how to define it, make sure you know how to apply it.
- The leadership dilemma shows that while culture is a clear priority, there is still some confusion around who is responsible. You may not be able to influence whether culture exists, but you can influence what kind of culture exists. Everyone is responsible for culture, but culture needs a leader.
- The skills dilemma highlights that there is an abundance of training, and yet an absence of confidence. With the right strategy and commitment, you can create the culture you want.

Try this

- Present the three dilemmas to your team, or take a moment to consider them personally. Which dilemma most resonates, and why? What roadblocks might these dilemmas create?
- Make a list of some of these roadblocks and work with your team to share ideas and strategies that will help you navigate them.

Work towards this

You and your team are aware of some of the challenges or roadblocks before you and have a clear plan for how you can address them.

Chapter 4

The conversations before the conversations

Start with your foundations

'There is no such thing as a worthless conversation, provided you know what to listen for. And questions are the breath of life for a conversation.' – James Nathan Miller

---

Key finding: More than 9 in 10 middle managers (95%) agree that culture is the outcome of little decisions made over time.

I've never considered myself a runner. If you've read my last book, *Lead the Room*, you would be familiar with the love-hate relationship I have with running. And yet, during the global pandemic, living in the world's most locked down city (not a title we are proud of), I couldn't help but feel compelled to get back into it. The real tipping point was walking to the top of the stairs in my house and my smart watch subtly tapping me on the wrist to say, 'Hey, it looks like you're working out'.

There's a common mistake I fell into when I first began that a lot of new runners make – trying to do too much, too fast after too little for too long. When I started running, I gave myself far more credit than my body had capability. I set out for my first run thinking 10 kilometres was a great place to start; after all, I had run a marathon in 2013, which was 42 kilometres. Almost immediately I knew I had made a huge mistake, and yet I decided to push through in the name of fitness. A subsequent week of shin splints and hobbling around my house almost convinced me that running really wasn't my thing.

David McHenry is a physiotherapist and strength coach to some of Nike's elite athletes, and he explains why running takes such a physical toll on the body:

'The average runner has to negotiate three to five times their body weight with each foot strike. If they're taking up to 90 foot strikes per foot per minute over the course of their run, that's an incredible amount of repetitive stress on the body.'

My enthusiasm for becoming a runner again outweighed my commitment to the process that was required to get there. I didn't fully understand that I was sabotaging my success by trying to do too much, too fast.

I changed my approach and committed to finishing each run with more in the tank. If I wanted to run seven or ten kilometres, and I knew I could, I intentionally pulled it back to three or five so I would come home feeling great instead of feeling depleted. Instead of chastising myself for not running at a faster pace, I listened to Nike's guided runs, which regularly told me to slow down and shifted my focus to practices such as mindfulness and gratitude during the run. While this might seem like an advertisement for Nike, I promise there's a point I'm trying to make here.

Parts Two and Three of this book centre on five practical conversations you can have with your team to help create the culture you want. They are simple conversations, but they sit on a foundation that takes time to build. The success of these conversations is set up by the conversations that precede them. I'm talking about your everyday, ordinary team conversations. Trying to tackle them without this foundation might just be doing a little too much, too fast after too little for too long. It might seem like a paradox to say that before you can have a culture conversation you need to have a culture of conversations, but that's essentially what I mean.

Conversation characteristics

So, what are some of the key characteristics you should be looking to build into your everyday discussions with your team to build your conversational capability? Here are five characteristics I would be looking to build into team conversations, and how you can do this.

Trust

Edelman is a global communications firm known for their research on trust in institutions over more than 20 years. While the world around us seems to be plagued by misinformation and mistrust, the 2021 *Edelman Trust Barometer* shows that business is not only the most trusted institution amongst the four studied – business, non-government organisations (NGOs), government and media – but it is also the only trusted institution globally. In Australia, 78 per cent trust 'my employer' over government (61 per cent) and the media (51 per cent). In many ways this is good news for people leaders, because Gallup's research has found that engagement increases sixfold when employees trust their organisation's leadership, and employees who trust their leaders are twice as likely to say they will be with their company one year from now.

What is concerning is that this trust doesn't necessarily run in both directions. A 2021 global research study of nearly 4000 employees and business leaders in 11 countries by The Workforce Institute at UKG found that 63 per cent of business leaders say trust must be earned, with just one in four leaders saying 'I trust you' on day one. When an employee feels that trust is lacking from their employer, it not only has the potential to erode the foundation of the relationship, but it affects productivity, mental health and turnover.

We need to be careful we don't hold onto a paradigm that people leaders can *presume* trust from their employees while the employees must *earn* trust from their leader. If anything, that paradigm is backwards. People leaders shouldn't presume trust from their employees but rather take the time to earn, build and maintain it. And in contrast, trust should be for the employee to lose rather than gain. According to the report *Trust in the Modern Workplace*, the good news about gaining trust is that the bar isn't set very high. While you might think trust is built through the more 'human' conversations such as discussing hobbies, passions and family life, the report found that sharing personal information was actually one of the least common ways both managers and team members build trust. According to their research, the most common ways a people leader can build and maintain the trust of their team members are to:

- be dependable (52 per cent)
- be honest (34 per cent)
- actively listen (28 per cent)
- give helpful feedback (25 per cent)
- model behaviours and lead by example (24 per cent)
- care about employee wellbeing (22 per cent).

Practically speaking, when it comes to the conversations in your team, you can reinforce trust by:

- following through on your commitments
- saying what you mean
- listening more than you speak
- making time for important conversations
- modelling what you talk about
- checking in with your people.

Vulnerability

'Vulnerability' is a word that has been amplified in business in recent years, in large part due to the incredible work of people such as Brené Brown, resulting in many people pushing for leaders to be more open and vulnerable with those people they lead. During the global pandemic, in moments of deep uncertainty, many of the clients I work with shared stories in which a leader's vulnerability rallied their people.

You may have heard the quote from Brené, 'Vulnerability sounds like truth and feels like courage. Truth and courage aren't always comfortable, but they're never weakness'. There's a much less commonly used quote from her on the topic from an interview with organisational psychologist Adam Grant on the TED podcast *WorkLife*: 'Vulnerability minus boundaries is not vulnerability'. In their conversation, she puts an important caveat upon how vulnerability is expressed at work. She draws an important distinction: 'Are you sharing your emotions and your experiences to move your work, connection or relationship forward? Or are you working your shit out with somebody? Work is not a place to do that'.

We admire the strength of others, but we connect through the vulnerability of others. But vulnerability needs clear boundaries. It does not mean airing your dirty laundry or working through your personal trauma at work. It is not a tool to use on your team; it is a personal practice. Vulnerability evokes vulnerability, but not when there is an agenda or expectation of something in return. As Patrick Lencioni writes in *The Advantage: Why Organizational Health Trumps Everything Else in Business*, leaders must go first:

> 'By taking the risk of making himself vulnerable with no guarantee that other members of the team will respond in kind, a leader demonstrates an extraordinary level of selflessness and dedication to the team. And that gives him the right, and the confidence, to ask others to do the same.'

Practically speaking, you can foster conversations with greater vulnerability in your team by:

· welcoming the hard conversations
· sharing with the right people when you are struggling
· speaking up when there is a misalignment of values
· being comfortable with not having all the answers
· admitting to your mistakes
· sharing personal but non-intrusive stories.

Empathy

As we live and lead in a world that can feel increasingly polarised, we need empathy now more than ever. As we navigate significant global change and disruption in the future of work, we can't lead effectively without it.

Businessolver has been evaluating the state of empathy in (American) workplaces and providing a report since 2017. Each year, more than 90 per cent of CEOs, HR managers and employees have agreed on the importance of empathy at work. In the 2021 report, 72 per cent of employees said that it's a key driver in employee motivation.

It might be tempting to dismiss it as a 'nice-to-have' skill, but the research shows it's a key factor in employee motivation, retention and delivering better business outcomes. It's a leadership imperative.

Empathy might be a soft skill but it's not fluffy. It's complex, demanding and strong. Empathy is not sympathy. Sympathy is pity for a person in their experience. Empathy allows us to sit with a person in their experience.

Empathy doesn't just feel *for* a person: it feels *with* them. Empathy helps us:

- sense the emotions of those around us
- surface the unspoken conversation in the room
- feel what they are feeling as though their feelings are our own
- see the world through their eyes and from their perspective.

You do not have to agree with a person's perspective. You may not necessarily condone the choices each person makes, but you are able to understand. This ability to understand is what makes empathy rich and powerful for leaders and teams.

In his MIT 2017 commencement speech, Apple CEO Tim Cook urged students: 'People will try to convince you that you should keep your empathy out of your career. Don't accept this false premise.'

We've come a long way in understanding the value of empathy, but we still have work to do. According to the *2021 State of Workplace Empathy* study, seven out of ten CEOs said it's hard for them to consistently demonstrate empathy in their working lives, and 68 per cent feared they would be less respected if they show empathy in the workplace.

Practically speaking, you can foster conversations with greater empathy in your team by:

- giving people the freedom to experience their emotions
- seeking to understand the emotions of others

- showing unconditional positive regard towards people
- finding common ground in shared experiences
- suspending judgement.

Curiosity

If there were just one behaviour you could adopt as a leader that would be most helpful and beneficial in your role, what would you choose? With more than 80 years of research on teams and organisations around the globe, Gallup suggests it's becoming more 'coach-like'. In fact, they identified the shift from 'boss' to 'coach' as one of six key changing demands of the modern workforce.

The shift from boss to coach is a shift of humility. It's an acknowledgement that you don't always have the answers and that there are times when you don't need to. It's also an acknowledgement that the answer you have may not always be the right answer or even the best one. In the words of Michael Bungay Stanier, bestselling author of *The Coaching Habit*, it's about 'stay[ing] curious a little longer. They're going to rush to action and advice-giving a little more slowly'.

I work with leaders as a coach and I train leaders to become more coach-like, so I've seen the enormous value of this skill in action. And yet, it always astounds me how many people I work with have never seen a coach-like approach to leadership modelled to them or have never had any training to become more coach-like in their role.

It shouldn't really come as a surprise, considering that most of our career we are rewarded and recognised – even promoted – for our ability to provide answers and solutions. People are regularly encouraged to 'come with answers or solutions' and celebrated when they do. So, with that in mind, it makes sense that we place an emphasis on 'having all the answers' when we step up into leadership. If we're honest with ourselves for a moment, it feels nice to be needed, which only reinforces the habit.

So, if we're not there to solve problems, then why are we the leader? As a leader you're there to develop problem-solvers. As validating as it might feel to give someone an answer, it's not even close to the satisfaction you'll feel helping them to discover that answer for themselves. As a leader, your goal is to focus less on having the best answers and more on asking the best questions. Coaching your team to think critically now will go a long way to helping them contribute meaningfully later.

Practically speaking, you can foster conversations with greater curiosity in your team by:

- avoiding being the first to share your ideas or thoughts
- asking more than you tell
- listening more than you speak
- encouraging external learning
- sharing diverse experiences
- celebrating critical thinking.

Safety

Back in 2008, a group of internal researchers at Google detailed ten characteristics that make a manager great. But they set out with a different hypothesis. For some of Google's technical engineers and leaders, managers were seen as 'at best a necessary evil, and at worst a useless layer of bureaucracy'. The researchers set out to prove that managers actually don't matter and that the quality of a manager didn't impact a team's performance. This hypothesis failed, and they learned that managers can have a significant impact on business outcomes and employee engagement. The ten characteristics Project Oxygen detailed included 'is a great coach', 'empowers team and does not micromanage' and 'is a good communicator – listens and shares information'.

Following the success of this research, Google researchers applied a similar method to uncover the secrets of effective teams. The project had the code name 'Project Aristotle', a tribute to Aristotle's quote, 'the whole is greater than the sum of its parts'. The Google researchers believed employees can do more working together than alone. What did they discover?

Of the five dynamics of effective teams that the researchers identified, psychological safety was by far the most important. This is how Google describes it:

> 'Psychological safety refers to an individual's perception of the consequences of taking an interpersonal risk or a belief that a team is safe for risk taking in the face of being seen as ignorant, incompetent, negative, or disruptive.'

Teams that fostered a sense of psychological safety were rated as effective twice as often by executive leaders, brought in more revenue to the business, saw greater diversity of ideas from within their teams and had members who were less likely to leave.

This held true in our research when we asked people leaders what evidence they look for of a healthy culture. The number-one area (62 per cent) was that 'team members feel safe to express their opinion'.

Practically speaking, you can foster conversations that are psychologically safe in your team by:

- avoiding being the first to share your ideas or thoughts
- encouraging your team to ask for help
- taking informed risks and supporting your team to do the same
- celebrating learning over punishment for failure
- inviting your team to disagree or challenge ideas
- acknowledging the input of others without interrupting
- leading with positive intent.

As a leader, you cannot presume trust, nor can you demand vulnerability. Trust needs to be built and maintained, and you must lead and demonstrate vulnerability and empathy. You also cannot take a conversation deeper than is psychologically safe, which is why curiosity and safety must operate hand in hand.

Every conversation you have with your team is an opportunity to build trust, lead vulnerability, show curiosity and create safety.

Find the missing voice

Culture conversations are collaborative conversations. But even with all the elements we've discussed present within a team, it's still possible that some voices will get lost in the conversation. It's your job as a leader to find the missing voice. All too often our best ideas, our most unique perspectives and our most innovative strategies in the meeting room die waiting behind a silent team member. I've spoken with those team members; I've been that team member. The *Harvard Business Review* article 'Can Your Employees Really Speak Freely?' states:

> '...when employees can voice their concerns freely, organizations see increased retention and stronger performance. At several financial services firms, for example, business units whose employees reported speaking up more had significantly better financial and operational results than others.'

As you embark on this series of conversations, it's important that you, as the leader, are intentional in amplifying the missing voice in the conversation. The loudest voice in the room isn't always right, and just because nobody is saying 'no' does not mean everybody is saying 'yes'.

There are some simple things that you can do that go a long way in bringing out the missing voice in the conversation:

1. **Wait a little longer:** We're mostly impatient. It's the consequence of having more items on the to-do list than we have space in the calendar. I understand that you want results, and you want them now so you can move on. Wait a little longer before you do. Learn to be comfortable with the moments of silence. Not everybody has an answer right away. In the silence, your team is processing what you have asked and thinking through their response. Move on too quickly and you might just miss what you really need.

2. **Look a little closer:** Who is contributing in the discussion? More importantly, who is not? Look a little closer at who is yet to speak. Engage, make eye contact, use their name and personally invite them to contribute to the conversation. Silence in the discussion does not mean an absence of something to contribute.

3. **Go a little deeper:** Ask the second question. How can you ask the same question in a different way? What is clear to some may not be clear to all. If people aren't responding, take time to go deeper and bring clarity. Use open questions and probing questions that seek to draw out meaningful answers rather than simple 'yes' or 'no' responses. Ask the follow-up question if you believe there is more to be uncovered.

4. **Speak a little slower:** It goes without saying that if you are speaking, your team is not. Be slow to speak in the room. Allow others to contribute first, even if you have a great answer. Don't rush to give your perspective until you've taken time to explore the other ideas in the room.

When you do hear that missing voice, be sure to affirm it, thank it and encourage it, even if it doesn't sound like yours. Every voice has something valuable to contribute.

Action steps

Remember this

- Start by building your foundations. Don't try to do too much, too fast after too little for too long. As a leader, you play a valuable role in ensuring that the foundation is strong.
- You can't presume trust. You must take the time to earn, build and maintain it.
- You can't demand vulnerability. You need to lead it with clear boundaries and without agenda.
- Empathy might be a soft skill, but it's not fluffy. It's complex, demanding and strong, and is needed now more than ever.
- Curiosity creates a shift from the leader being 'the problem-solver' to having a team of problem-solvers.
- Your conversations can only go as deep as they are psychologically safe.
- Every conversation you have with your team is an opportunity to build trust, lead vulnerability and empathy, show curiosity and create safety.

Try this

- Reflect on the five areas of trust, vulnerability, empathy, curiosity and psychological safety, and discuss the following questions with your team:
  - How would we rate our conversations in relation to these key characteristics?
  - What do we do well?
  - What could we do better?
  - What will we do about that?
- Introduce some non-intrusive personal questions to get to know your team better and build trust at your team meetings.

- Instead of rushing to give answers, try to coach more often.
- Regularly invite your team to challenge ideas or share their thoughts.
- Introduce an ideas exchange, where people share what they have been reading or learning.

Work towards this

This is not an overnight outcome. It is a regular commitment to ensure these characteristics are present in your team communication.

PART TWO

CULTURE
CONVERSATIONS

Culture is an abstract concept, but that doesn't mean it can't be practical. That's the focus of this section. We're going to start with three of the five culture conversations that you can have with your team to start to shape a culture by design right now.

In conversation one, we look at some of the unseen elements of culture and learn how you can start to make the unspoken expectations of yourself and your team more explicit.

In conversation two, we learn how to make the unseen elements of culture more observable through behaviours, so you and your team know what these expectations look like in reality and can live them out day to day.

In conversation three, we explore how to incorporate these cultural expectations and behaviours into the everyday vocabulary of your team through a shared language.

To end Part Two, we look at a practical way you can prioritise, maintain visibility and measure your progress.

Chapter 5

The expectation conversation

Make the unspoken spoken

'What isn't communicated, is felt. What is felt, is interpreted. What is interpreted is often inaccurate.' – Tory Eletto

---

Key finding: Almost half of people leaders (49%) strongly agree that their organisation's values are clearly communicated to everyone, but just 3 in 10 strongly agree their leaders demonstrate those organisational values.

I want you to think about a time when you were disappointed. Don't think about it for too long. What happened? I may not know the specifics of your situation, but at a higher level I can likely predict what took place. At some point in the lead-up to the moment, you had an expectation of how something would go, but the reality didn't live up to that expectation. Perhaps it was something you bought that you thought would transform your life and it didn't. Or it was a movie that didn't live up to the hype. Or maybe it was a vision of what you thought a promotion would entail, and it turned out nothing like you had imagined.

Whether we are always conscious of them or not, we live our lives with certain expectations: expectations about ourselves, such as who we should be or what we should be doing; expectations about others, such as who they should be and how they should treat us; and expectations about the world in general, such as what the world should do for us or be. They may not be written down and we may not always be able to articulate them, but internally we all carry a set of expectations of how we would prefer things to be, which informs our actions and responses. Imagine a small, inbuilt and invisible rule book that we use to govern our lives (and secretly judge others against). Most people unconsciously live life according to their own rule book and assume that others are living by it too. They are not.

For some people, the idea of not being able to follow through on a work commitment they made leaves them feeling sick in the stomach. How can they not deliver on something they said 'yes' to? Their internal expectation of self is that their word is their bond, and so they do everything they can – even at times to their own detriment – to deliver on their promise. When a colleague makes a commitment, that expectation is immediately placed upon them, too. The problem is that this isn't always a shared expectation. This clash of expectations can lead to confusion, conflict and straight-up frustration in a team, because we have different players playing the same game according to a different set of unspoken rules.

What are your expectations around strategy? Is it best done alone or together? Should strategy be collaborative or dictated? What about relationships at work – do we talk about life outside of work or keep it strictly professional? How should people handle conflict? How much autonomy should people have? What is the appetite for failure on your team? You might think the answers are obvious. They are not. As a leader, you have expectations of your team and they have expectations of you. On top of all of this, your organisation has a set of expectations of you too, which is usually reflected in your company values or mission.

Take a moment to think about the qualities of your ideal team. If you woke up tomorrow and your team was everything you wanted it to be, what words would you use to describe it? Grab a pen and paper and draw five lines, or open a note on your phone, and write down the first five words that come to mind.

I've done this exercise with a broad range of teams, and I usually hear words like 'optimistic', 'passionate', 'positive', 'courageous', 'honest', 'collaborative', 'connected', 'encouraging' and 'innovative'. Take a moment to reflect on the words you chose and then answer this next question truthfully:

When was the last time you told your team this?

If you're like many of the people leaders I talk to, the answer is usually 'Not recently'. We know that culture has an unseen element that typically incorporates things such as values, beliefs, understandings and meanings, which inform our behaviours. Our goal in this first conversation is to uncover what is unseen and surface the unspoken expectations so that they are clear and explicit to those around us. Only once we talk about those expectations can we understand them and determine whether or not they serve us or the team.

Clarification helps lower the waterline – a conversation with Beth

Beth recently finished in her role working as Head of People and Experience at one of Australia's largest retailers, known for its fashion and stationery brands. With 1300 stores in 22 countries, the business employs over 18,000 people.

As a business that has been operating for over 30 years, for 29 of those years the culture was largely unspoken. Beth told me:

'It was implied. It's experiential. We had the values, we had the vision, all of those things, but we hadn't really captured our culture.'

After a number of discussions, and after coming across the famous Netflix culture deck, they recognised that they needed to do something that helped people to attach to the organisation and support 'the speed to competency', because their new people were spending so much time trying to figure out why they did things the way they did them:

'We used to call it "the secret herbs and spices". And then it was like, why are they even secret? Can we just actually spend the time to articulate our culture so that people know what they're buying into in terms of the recruitment process, and that people during their induction are getting sticky quicker and speed to competency is quicker, because they get it. They get the playing field.'

From this discussion, the organisation developed their own culture document:

'It is what we call our culture and essentially they're character-istics that we live by. So whilst our values are what we believe in, our characteristics, and specifically [the culture document], essentially make up the way that plays out culturally.'

By intentionally verbalising these characteristics, the team was able to make the unspoken elements of culture more explicit for their people:

'You think about culture as being that good old iceberg in terms of what is above versus below the waterline. We've lowered the waterline through using the language. It's not hidden anymore. It's out there. Everybody can see it; everybody talks about it. I can actually hook onto this, because I actually get it and I understand it and I know what it means.'

'Lowering the waterline' is a powerful metaphor for what happens when leaders are able to make the unspoken spoken. It helps each person understand and align around what is expected, and in the process, everybody benefits:

'Even our executive team were like, "Why didn't someone give me this document when I started? It would've helped so much of my mental anguish trying to figure out why we do things the way we do things". So it really aligned 18,000 people around words.'

This commitment to culture helped set the organisation apart from their competition and not only survive COVID-19 but thrive, when many global retailers crumbled under lockdowns and restrictions. Beth shared a powerful example of their culture in action:

'When they closed the stores, there were many retailers that just focused on their online business and left their products in stores, waiting patiently to find out when they could trade. We had team members without being asked... with no direction from the group, going to their stores and packing up boxes to reverse-engineer our logistics so that they could feed our online store, so that we could continue trading. And in doing so, they not only fed our top line, but also it meant that when we opened our store, we weren't sitting there with aged, old-looking stock. We actually could replenish all of our stock in our stores and show up versus the competition as having the newness and the on-trend and the seasonally relevant product.

'Those middle managers are the ones that switched overnight [to], "Okay, I'm no longer in the brick business, I'm in the online business; how do I feed this online store?" And for many of them they actually went and worked at our distribution centres in order to be able to fuel the growth that was happening across that channel.'

By making their culture explicit and clarifying the culture, the business was able to lower the waterline so people were clear on their expectations and understood what they were empowered to do. Beth cites the culture as something that empowered their people leaders to step up in a moment of need. The culture document is valued so highly by their team that they see it as a source of competitive advantage, and because of that it's not possible for me to share any more of the specific details.

Finding the core

One of the big questions people leaders asked in our research was, 'How do I get people on board with culture?' The most obvious answer is to start by including them in the conversation. Your culture is not something to go away and create and bring back for your team. It's something to build in collaboration with your team. In 2012, the UK Department of Health released a document titled *Liberating the NHS*, which outlined their plan to put patients first and give everyone more say over their care and treatment by ensuring they were part of the conversation. They used the language 'No decision about me, without me' to carry the campaign. This is a helpful way to approach the conversation about culture. If you're going to make an important decision about the way you work together with your team, don't do it without them.

In the first conversation with your team, you are going to explore three sets of expectations. You are trying to identify the expectations that align you. These core expectations are what bind you together and help your team to be at its best. Think about the core as what sits at the intersection of 'you', 'them' and 'us':

- **'You' as a people leader:** What are the expectations you have of your team and of the organisation?
- **'Them' as a team member:** What are your team's expectations of you and the organisation?
- **'Us' as an organisation:** What are the organisation's expectations of us collectively?

How well defined your organisational values or culture are will differ between organisations; however, if you find yourself in a position of leadership in your current organisation, I can only assume that there is at least some degree of overlap between your personal expectations of the organisation and its expectations of you. People leaders who don't have some kind of alignment are either unlikely to be recruited for the role or unlikely to stay in the role. The same could be said of your team and their relationship to the organisation.

If you think about the relationship between you, your team and the organisation as a Venn diagram, we are seeking to bring these three independent and unique parts together to identify what we share in common. As you enter the conversation with more intention and curiosity, you can discover more of this core that unites people.

Figure 2: You, your team and the organisation

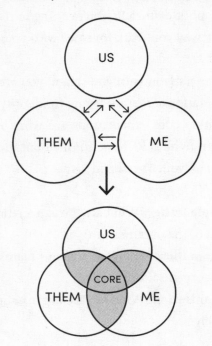

You might think that your goal as a leader should be to grow the core by increasing the overlap. Great culture must mean closing the Venn so that it becomes one unified circle, right? Pause. That's not my advice here.

When building your ideal team culture, your aim is not to morph people into some beige homogeneous blob where each person thinks, talks and acts the same. You are not a mini version of the company, and your team does not need to be another you. If you aim for that, you rob yourselves of the many powerful benefits of your differences and diversity, such as innovation, perspective and progress.

It's OK to disagree. It's OK to have your differences. You actually need them and you're better for them. As a Gallup-Certified Strengths Coach, I get the privilege of seeing the power of differences on a regular basis when working with teams.

In 2017 I was working with a small team at a great Australian startup which was in the business of serving small businesses. You'd be hard-pressed to find a founder or CEO more passionate and energetic about their organisation's mission than theirs. While the company was relatively small at the time, his vision for having locations across Australia was without a doubt one of the driving forces for the progress they had made. I wasn't surprised to learn that his top CliftonStrengths (a tool Gallup developed to identify themes of talent) were 'Futuristic' and 'Activator'. People with a high Futuristic theme are, as the name suggests, 'inspired by the future and what could be'. They 'energise others with their visions of the future'. This was coupled with the Activator theme, which is characterised as having the ability to 'make things happen by turning thoughts into action'. They 'want to do things now rather than simply talk about them'. These themes summed him up perfectly. The challenge was the founder's relationship with the CFO. People called him 'the NO man'. He had a reputation for pushing back on decisions and slowing things down. When we started to unpack his strengths, we learned that he was high in the Deliberative theme. This theme is characterised 'by the serious care they take in making decisions or choices' and the way they 'anticipate obstacles'. Interestingly, the CFO was the only person in the team who had this theme. While Activators have tended to be described as a 'foot on the accelerator', Deliberative people are more often seen as the 'foot on the brake'.

Despite the previous conflict they had experienced around these contrasting themes, this difference is a huge advantage. The founder's strengths allow him to cast a compelling vision for the future, while the CFO ensures they make decisions that enable them to be around long enough to experience that future. Differences are advantages.

What stood out in this experience for me was that both the founder and the CFO were aligned at the core. They both wanted the same thing. They both wanted to feel excited about the future. But what helped them to do that looked different. One needed to look at the future; the other needed to understand the facts. One needed to see the opportunities and the other needed to be aware of the obstacles. When they were able to leverage each other's differences around a common core, it transformed how they were able to work together.

Building a winning team culture is about being aligned at the core and ensuring you remain inclusive at the edges.

Having the conversation

Let's get super practical. As you facilitate this first conversation with your team, you might find it helpful to think about it taking place in four parts: naming, framing, exploring and reframing.

1. Naming the expectations

In the first part of the conversation, we're going to share and capture.

Start the conversation by discussing your organisation. This gives people the time to get into a conversational flow before anyone needs to share personally. Take a moment with your team to reflect on your organisation's purpose, mission and values. If your organisation has already done the work to make your culture explicit, be sure to include that in the conversation. What are some of the key expectations the organisation has of you as an individual and as a team? Once you have discussed expectations from an organisational perspective, shift the focus onto your team and ask them to reflect on their own expectations of the organisation and of each other. Then, once your team has had an opportunity to share, you can share your own. Your ability to stay curious and not judgmental, along with your ability to ask great questions, is what will set this conversation up for success.

Below are a few questions you could ask your team to stimulate the conversation.

About the organisation, you could ask:

· Which of our organisation's values most align with your own?
· What words would you use to describe the best parts of our organisation's culture?
· What expectations does our organisation have of this team?
· If our executive team were here, what would they say are the ideal qualities of a team?

About you and the team, you could ask:

· What are your top personal values?
· What is important to you on a team?
· What do you expect from the organisation?
· What do you expect from me as this team's leader?
· What do you expect of each other?
· What are the ideal qualities of a team from your perspective?
· What is something you would like this team to be known for?

If you're struggling to find new ideas, you could try asking:

· When was a time you didn't enjoy working in a team?
· What has frustrated you in the past working in a team?

From here you can positively reframe the challenges or frustrations to better understand what each person holds in high esteem.

To deepen the answers you and your team share, it can be helpful to explore the questions through the lens of an external third party. Try asking questions like the following:

· If someone came in and observed us at our best, what qualities would they be able to notice?

- If someone followed us around for a week and observed the way we communicate, connect and collaborate, what words would they use to describe this team?

As a facilitator of the conversation, imagine you are holding your team up in front of everyone like a diamond and shining a light through it as you rotate it. Each twist and turn of the diamond reveals something new and unique about it. Take time to capture the answers, knowing that you may end up with big and abstract expectations or small and concrete examples; make sure you capture both. There are no wrong answers.

As you listen to the perspectives, you'll need to find a way to capture these ideas in a way that is visible to the room. In person, this could be a whiteboard or wall of Post-it Notes (yes, exactly like the stereotypical team brainstorm session). Online there are a number of great digital tools that can be used to both capture and present participant responses.

Here are a few practical tips for capturing the conversation:

- Go fast enough to keep the conversation flowing but slow enough to really listen to the responses.
- Capture their words, not your summary of them.
- If you're not sure what they mean, clarify, don't interpret. Ask, don't assume.
- Keep seeking out the unspoken conversation in the room and invite the quiet voices to contribute.

2. Framing the expectations

In the second part of the conversation, we're grouping and chunking.

One of the reasons capturing the ideas and making them visible is so important is that it enables you and your team to take a step back and begin to group these expectations into themes.

As you and your team look at what was shared, take a moment to reflect:

- What do the expectations we have discussed have in common?
- What themes have emerged from what we have shared?
- If we could describe an expectation in just a few words, what words would we choose?
- What is this all really about?

You will find the concept of 'chunking up' helpful in this part of the conversation. Chunking is a linguistic tool used by neuro-linguistic programming (NLP) practitioners to help clients move between differing degrees of abstraction. American physicist Richard P. Feynman referred to these abstractions as 'the hierarchy of ideas'.

If we become aware of the varying degrees of abstraction and this hierarchy, it allows us to chunk up or down depending on what is required at each stage of the conversation. Let's take a look at an example to better understand this in action.

Depending on your goal, you could move up or down through different levels of specificity. If you're talking about a car and choose to move down a layer, you might choose to talk about a brand of car, such as a Kia, or a Mercedes-Benz, or a Ferrari. Go down another layer and you might talk more specifically about the model, such as a Kia Cerato or a Mercedes-Benz A-Class. Go down another layer and you could discuss parts and components, such as the tyres or steering wheel, which again could chunk down to rubber or other materials. In contrast, if we decide to chunk up, we could step up from car to transportation. Another layer up from transportation is travel, or even a much more abstract concept such as movement or energy.

At this stage of the conversation, it's OK for the concepts to be higher in their degree of abstraction. Going higher in the hierarchy allows us find commonality in our ideas with a greater degree of ease.

Figure 3: Chunking up and down

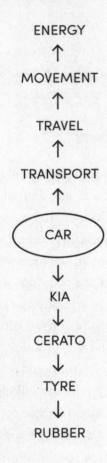

ENERGY

↑

MOVEMENT

↑

TRAVEL

↑

TRANSPORT

↑

CAR

↓

KIA

↓

CERATO

↓

TYRE

↓

RUBBER

Consider these example expectations:

- In our ideal team, we ask about life outside of work.
- Our organisation values a people-centred approach.
- I value my team talking to me when they are struggling.

Each response sits at a different level of abstraction, and yet if we chunk up we can see some common themes. When we ask, 'What is this really about?', we could identify that what connects these expectations is that people want to work in a team that feels *relational*. Or maybe what we all have in common is that we want to work in a culture that feels *connected*.

As you begin to chunk up, you will be surprised to see just how much your team's expectations of self, others and the business have in common. These words can help frame your expectations.

3. Exploring the expectations

In the third part of the conversation, we are investigating and evaluating.

Holly Ransom is one of Australia's most impressive young entrepreneurs and leaders. In 2012 the *Australian Financial Review* included her as one of their '100 Australian Women of Influence', making her the youngest person to receive the honour. She is known as one of the world's top keynote speakers, CEO of her own company and author of the book *The Leading Edge*. She has spent a decade studying leadership and has had the privilege of interviewing incredible luminaries including Barack Obama, Condoleezza Rice, Sir Richard Branson, Malcolm Gladwell and Simon Sinek. In a conversation with Holly on my podcast, she shared a moment with a mentor that had a big impact on her. She recounts the story in her book *The Leading Edge*:

> 'John turned up to coffee and placed a dice in the middle of the table. I was intrigued. "What do you see?" John asked. I couldn't work out what his angle was, so I gave the direct response: "A dice." "Be more specific," he pushed me. "I can see a three," I said. John replied, "Well, I can see a four. Which of us is right?" Of course, we both were. "Bingo," he said. "One of the most important lessons for you to learn early in your career and cultivate into a habit is being intentional about the diversity of perspectives in helping to inform your view of the whole.'

In our conversation, she shared this story with one more insight. She told me, 'Just because your perspective is right does not mean it's the only one'.

Of course, just because we hold certain expectations of ourselves and the world, that doesn't mean those expectations are right. If we are going to have a conversation about expectations, it's important that this conversation takes time to investigate and evaluate those expectations and determine whether or not they serve us or the collective. For some of the people on your team, this will be the first time they have verbalised these unspoken expectations.

It's important to note that 'investigating' and 'evaluating' are words that evoke a sense of curiosity and exploration, and not judgement or criticism. In many ways, our thoughts and beliefs can feel like truth until we are given the opportunity to challenge them. I think about it like an internal lawyer tasked with a cross-examination. A witness can appear to be telling the whole truth until they are challenged. Everything can seem true until it gets put under the microscope. American jurist and law expert John Henry Wigmore described cross-examination as 'the best legal engine ever created for the discovery of truth'.

As you surface the unspoken expectations of your team, your goal is not to disprove or discredit but to safely cross-examine, investigate and evaluate.

Take a moment to ask these important questions about the themes which emerge:

- Are these expectations helpful?
- How do these expectations serve our team or business?
- Are these expectations logical and fair?
- Can we truly live up to these expectations?

For example, a team member or leader may have surfaced an expectation for the team to be conflict-free. Is this a realistic expectation?

Is there a more helpful way we could express this? If so, you will need to reframe the expectation.

4. Reframing the expectations

In the final part of the conversation, we are choosing and documenting.

Once you have determined the key themes that have emerged from the conversation, this is an opportunity to reframe these in a way that best serves you and your team. For now, try to keep each theme to one or two words to make it easy to remember and capture.

By the end of this conversation, you should be able to articulate a number of the key unspoken expectations of you, your team and the organisation and group these into key themes. Ideally you would be aiming to keep the number of themes to around five to seven. In order to do this, you will need your team to agree on the themes that are most important to them. You can ask your team to vote on the themes or find a way that best suits you to choose.

Try asking your team the following questions:

- If you could pick just one or two of these words to describe the team you want, which would you choose?
- Which of these themes most resonates with you?
- If our team embodied one of these themes, which would make the biggest difference?

If you're thinking that these core expectations resemble a set of team values, that's a valid point. Values really are just chunked-up expectations. They are what we hold in high regard or esteem. But I've intentionally steered away from using that language because I don't want you to see them as a replacement to the hard work your organisation has done in creating company values or culture. These chunked-up expectations serve a very specific purpose, which we will learn about in the next few conversations.

Once you have your answers, find a way to document these. Now you're ready to get started on conversation number two: the clarification conversation.

Action steps

Remember this

- Culture has an unseen element.
- We all carry an unspoken set of expectations of how we would prefer things to be, which informs our actions and responses.
- The expectation conversation is about making the unspoken spoken – taking the time to surface these unspoken expectations we have of each other and that the organisation has of us to discover what we value and hold in high regard as a team.
- Making these expectations clear helps lower the waterline – that is, make more of the culture visible.
- If you want people to buy into the culture, include them in the conversation.

Try this

Schedule some time with your team to have the expectation conversation:

- Name the expectations: find the core themes by asking your team members the following questions:
  - What do you expect of the team?
  - What do you expect of me and each other?
  - What does the organisation expect of us?
  Share and capture the responses of the team. Capture their words, not your summary. Make the ideas visible.

- Frame the expectations: find what these expectations have in common by chunking up and grouping. You could ask the following questions:
  - What do these expectations have in common?
  - What themes have begun to emerge here?
- Explore the expectations: investigate and evaluate whether these themes are helpful and whether or not they serve the culture you are trying to create.
- Reframe the expectations: choose the themes that most resonate with the culture you're trying to create. Keep each theme to one or two words to make it easy to remember.
- Collaboratively decide on five to seven key themes that are most important to the team and document them for the next conversation.

Work towards this

By the end of this conversation, you should have something that looks like Figure 4 overleaf. Note that it lists just three expectation themes, rather than five to seven, however.

Figure 4: Example results of the expectation conversation

Collaboration	Connection	Creativity
We make quick decisions	Unified	Think differently
People are positive	Trusting	Learn from failure
We share information	We have a clear vision	Growth mindset
Outcomes-oriented	People care about each other	Modern thinking
Communicative	Empowering	Open
Reliable	We tell the truth	Proactive
Challenging	Be real with each other	
Hard working		
Take accountability		
Strengths-focused		

Chapter 6

The clarification conversation

Make the invisible observable

'Determine what behaviors and beliefs you value as a company, and have everyone live true to them. These behaviors and beliefs should be so essential to your core, that you don't even think of it as culture.' – Brittany Forsyth, VP of Human Relations, Shopify

---

Key finding: Only 36% of people leaders strongly agree that their organisational values are more than words and that the behavioural expectations are clearly defined.

A single word can have a multitude of meanings. Take the two-letter word, 'Ah'.

Try saying it out loud. How did you interpret it? Now say it like:

- you've just sat down after a long day on your feet
- you're contemplating a decision

- you've just seen a typo you made on an all-staff email
- you're watching fireworks go off
- you've just kicked your little toe on the edge of the couch
- you've just walked into your surprise party
- you've just had someone cut in line in front of you.

Do you get the point?

I'm never surprised when we experience miscommunication in the home or workplace. Communication is complex. I have learned (at times the hard way) that just because I am speaking, it doesn't always mean I am being heard. It's possible for people to listen to my words and yet completely miss what I'm trying to say, and the same is no doubt true for you. When my wife says, 'Hey, let's eat dinner at the table instead of the couch', I've learned that those words are less about where we are eating our meal and more about what we are doing while we eat.

If a single word can have a multitude of meanings, it's worth taking the time to ensure you've got the right word. So, how do we reduce the likelihood of miscommunication when it comes to culture?

Clarify, don't interpret

The goal of communication isn't just to exchange words – it's to transfer meaning. We want to know, 'Did you really understand what I meant?' When we feel understood, we feel seen and heard.

You might know from this book or my last that I'm an author, trainer, coach, speaker and facilitator. I'm also a runner, a creative and a very bad dancer.

What you might not know is that I'm also a trained counsellor.

I don't choose to practice or work as a counsellor because I've learned that I prefer the role of coach over therapist, although many of the skills and concepts I learned in counselling have been invaluable in what I do now. One of those skills that has been transformational for me, not only as a coach but in life in general, has been the art of asking better questions. After writing my first book, *Lead the Room*, which almost entirely focused on using speaking as a tool to mobilise people behind your ideas, I was asked to contribute my number-one piece of advice for another author's book on communication. I reflected deeply, and what I shared was: 'Good leaders know how to speak; great leaders know when not to'. It's important that leaders know how to communicate their ideas, but it's imperative that they know how to ask great questions and then shut up and listen. As a counsellor, I was taught the importance of asking clarifying questions to ensure that what you were hearing from the client was what they actually meant. The value of this cannot be overstated.

Imagine a person on your team came to you right now and told you they were 'stressed'. How would you interpret that? It might mean that they need some additional support to get their work done. It might also mean that they have something happening at home and need to take some time off. It could also mean they are depleted and about to resign. Without clarifying, you cannot appropriately respond to the need in front of you.

If you can't define it, you won't recognise it

From our understanding of culture, we know that there is an observable element. We can see culture expressed in sets of behaviours, systems, practices, patterns and ways of doing things. It shows up in the ways we act and respond and communicate.

At the end of the expectation conversation, you will have surfaced some of the unspoken expectations in your team and 'chunked up' to identify some of the key themes that align you at the core. What the first conversation won't leave you with is *how* these themes are outworked and observed day to day. One of the big criticisms you will often hear about organisational values is that people are not always able to identify exactly how these values are lived practically. The values, while meaningful, are usually so abstract that they live on a wall and not in the daily actions of the people. In our research we asked people leaders how much they agree with this statement:

Our values are clearly communicated to everyone.

Just under half of people (49 per cent) strongly agreed with this statement. When it came to being able to describe the organisation's values and how they are lived out every day, just 39 per cent of people leaders strongly agreed. But when it came to the statement 'our organisational values are more than words, the behavioural expectations are clearly defined', just 36 per cent of leaders strongly agreed.

What we learned from our research is that when people leaders work in organisations that promote a shared understanding of behavioural expectations, they have a much clearer reference point when it comes to addressing cultural inconsistencies down the track. Clarifying the observable behaviours makes it easier to shape the culture you want, and not just for you as a leader. The people leaders who were most effective at addressing cultural inconsistencies were those that developed the accepted behaviours collaboratively with their team based on their organisational values:

'We see developing behavioural expectations as an all-of-team thing. We put together a culture charter a couple of years ago, but we got input from everyone. We had a whole day in which the team split into different groups, and they came up with "dos" and "don'ts" for each of our five values. Everyone came in with their ideas, which then got taken to the management team, and we refined it. Then we went back to everyone and presented the culture charter to them, and explained why some things were included and some things weren't.

'I think it's very important if you ask for people's input that you don't ignore it. It creates a kind of anti-culture. We use that culture charter if something comes up that makes us think, "Something doesn't feel right" – we go back, have a look and ask, "Is this in line?" It helps us frame conversations with people when they start behaving in a way that is not in line with our culture. That is something we decided to do a few years ago, to put something more formal in place. Before that we just went by the vibe.'

When behavioural expectations are developed collaboratively, it helps everyone on your team to understand the culture, and most importantly, it leads to a shared accountability among people. Put simply, when people know how to define the culture, they know what they need to aim for. They'll recognise it when they see it lived out, and they will call it out when it's not.

I think it's important to mention again that the goal of the expectation conversation is not to provide you with a new list of team values to put on your wall or on the bottom of your email signature. It's to identify a set of shared core expectations that you can then use to guide this clarification conversation.

Culture is a set of observable behaviours

Dan Mottau is an experienced organisational development leader with a wealth of experience working in a broad range of well-known technology companies, including Zendesk, Redbubble and ZipCo. He draws on his experience and the principles of behavioural psychology and anthropology to cultivate psychologically safe and productive workplaces and enhance team performance. When it comes to the conversation about culture, he holds a very strong view about the role of behaviours in the success of culture:

'Values will not equal culture, ever. At least, that's my opinion. Values are a threshhold for entry, not the road to culture and high performance. And that's the biggest mistake I think people make, which is they try to change or use the values as that vehicle and mechanism. But the problem with values, again, is it's how we fundamentally believe. And let's also be honest: most values are pretty binary and foundational. It's, "Are you an accountable human being? Do you trust people? Are you empathetic and caring?" If you're not doing those things, you're not even a functioning human being, frankly. Values are not the destination.'

The point Dan makes is a valuable one, and one that applies to our conversation about the unseen elements of culture. They are pieces of the puzzle and not the puzzle itself. They need to be viewed through the lens of the process. Here's why:

'Values are not, by nature, behaviourally defined. And that's the biggest problem: if you can't define it and see it, then you can't measure and reinforce or shift it. You certainly won't be able to shift it over a short period of time. So, it isn't going to have the desired effect. And that ain't culture.'

It's important to remember that the goal of the clarification conversation is to make the invisible observable. Dan shared with me a powerful explanation of why values are not enough and must be partnered with explicit and measurable behaviours:

'[Take] two of the common values: accountability and bold-ness. Let's say you're a software engineer and you build the most whiz-bang app that nobody ever asked for. That's not bold, because you're not also being accountable and balanced.

'You can do the dumbest shit in the world and say, well, you're doing it because you are bold. And it could result in an incredible waste of time and resources, or even damage the company's reputation if it slips into production. And it's, again, why I don't think values are typically helpful. Saying "Be bold!", well, people can interpret that a million ways… I'm not saying constrain people, but what I'm saying is have focused behaviours that are explicit, measurable and definable, and also contextualised for the work that you're doing. And there-fore, the priorities of the team and the goals of the team – and the behaviours that go with them – live side by side. And you achieve your objectives through the interplay between those behaviours. And the culture is just the output of how that all went down.'

When it comes to your core expectations, just like values, it isn't enough to simply say, 'This is what we expect of each other,' or, 'This is what we value on this team'. The expectations need clarification, and the most helpful way to clarify them is to make the behaviours explicit.

Cisco's conscious culture

Headquartered in San Jose, California, Cisco is a worldwide leader in IT and networking, transforming how people connect, communicate and collaborate. With over 74,000 employees worldwide and 10,000 people leaders across 480 offices in 100-plus countries, Cisco was number one on the 'World's Best Workplaces' list by Great Places to Work and *Fortune* magazine in both 2019 and 2020. I had the opportunity to connect with James Comer, who is the Head of

People and Communities, Australia and New Zealand, to talk about the extensive work the organisation has undertaken to build an exceptional workplace culture. The team at Cisco describe it as their 'conscious culture', James explained:

> 'For me, conscious culture has really been about doing exactly what you're researching, Shane. It's being purposeful about the characteristics and environmental elements that come together to form your experience of work. When we say something's conscious, you're doing something with intent. You're doing something because you know you can have influence. You're doing something because you know that when you take an action, it is serving to reinforce the culture that you're trying to build, and that's why the term of "stewardship" for me is really important. It is that leaders, no matter where in the organisation they exist, understand that when they say something, when they behave in a particular way, they are contributing to or detracting from our culture, and we hope that they do more of the former than the latter. And that's what we really try and work with them on: helping them understand what it means to be a conscious leader.'

In order to empower each person in the organisation to be more conscious of the culture and their role in shaping it, Cisco needed to ensure that the expectations were clear. This was a process that was led from the top by CEO Chuck Robbins and the executive leadership team. But more importantly, it was a process that was developed and built from the bottom up by its employees. It was created intentionally from feedback received by Cisco employees about the kind of environment that would support their individual and collective success.

This conscious culture was a process built on something known internally as the 'people deal'. The people deal defines what Cisco employees can expect to receive from the company, and then outlines what Cisco expects in return from its employees. This conscious culture ensures each employee is able to observe and be more aware of the organisation's cultural expectations or principles, feel personally accountable for maintaining and improving the Cisco culture, and act appropriately when they see behaviour that is in alignment or misalignment with the culture. James explained:

'Intention's a great word. Conscious culture is being deliberate in your behaviour – how you show up, how you speak, or even in what you don't do or say. We know that intention is important. We know that intention is such a powerful element in what people value at Cisco and what makes us a great place to work. It's also important that everybody recognises they have a responsibility to keep it that way, and it's really easy to pat people on the back, high five, give them rewards [and] recognition when they exhibit behaviours that are consistent or go above and beyond.

'Where the challenge is, is when you see things that don't align with or advance your culture. That's where the preservation, the growth and the evolution of culture really kicks in, and everybody in this company has a responsibility to feel like they can put their hand up and should put their hand up when they see something that doesn't align, there is a safe mechanism for people to call out misalignment, and a dialogue to understand what we're doing about it. When those discussions and those situations become hard, we want our people to know that you can call it out with confidence, that we've got a mechanism and channels and safe processes that you can use for us to be able to work with you and figure out how we address it.'

Clarification of which behaviours should be confronted and which should be rewarded is essential. James commented on this from a leadership perspective:

> 'We know that one of the big parts of what culture is, is behaviours. It's understanding how your behaviours and your decisions impact those around you, and we can blow that up in a number of different ways, but an example of that is having awareness about how your intentions can be perceived – you might communicate with a particular intention, but how that is perceived can be affected by other people's reality. So, being a conscious leader is understanding that your behaviours, your words are having an interpreted impact. So, being a conscious leader is really about understanding how your role as a leader impacts and influences and motivates – or not – other people around you.'

Cisco has undertaken a significant amount of work to determine which behaviours produce the best outcomes for a team from a global perspective. In previous years, just 16 per cent of employees were fully engaged at Cisco; now, more than half of their people would be classified as fully engaged. Cisco's global teams study found eight factors that differentiated their best from the rest. These included the following:

1. **Purpose:** I am really enthusiastic about the mission of my company.
2. **Shared understanding of excellence:** In my team, I am surrounded by people who share my values.
3. **Safety and support:** My team mates have my back.
4. **Communication and leadership confidence:** I have great confidence in my company's future.

5. **Alignment:** At work I clearly understand what is expected of me.
6. **Best of me now:** I have a chance to use my strengths every day at work.
7. **Attention to me:** I know I will be recognised for excellent work.
8. **Best of me in the future:** In my work, I am always challenged to grow.

Once Cisco was able to clarify the behaviours of their top teams, it was then able to create a series of rituals that would help leaders replicate what the best teams did in order to replicate their best teams. Being a technology company, it even created a tool to support these rituals called Team Space. James shared a couple of examples of these rituals that Team Space enabled:

'First and foremost, our leaders pay weekly attention to their team members. Okay, nothing new there, right? One of the things that we firmly believe is that people don't want feedback. They want attention. And the narrative there is that when you ask someone, "Hey, can I give you some feedback?", every orifice in their body puckers up and they go into defence mode, right? But when you pay them regular attention that is centred on their strengths, the conversation becomes a more natural dialogue along the lines of, "Here are the things that you did really well, and this is how you played to your strengths", and, "Hey, here are some areas that we could probably work on together", and shift into more of a growth mindset conversation.

'So, every week we ask our team members to check in through Team Space with their leader, and it asks them a series of consistent questions: What did you love about what you did last week? What did you loathe about what you did last week? Do you feel you added value last week? What are your priorities for this week, and what do you need from your leader to make this next week successful? So, not only does that help our people talk regularly to their leader about how they are or are not playing to their strengths, not only does it help them make sure that their values and focus and priorities' alignment is there, but the tool also registers when that check-in has been submitted, and it tells the employee when that check-in's been viewed by their leader, and any comments they have left. So, they know that their leader has paid attention to it.

'And then... typically when the attention is paid to them through a one-on-one, it changes the conversation. You don't spend the first 15, 20, half an hour talking to your leader about what you loved about your work last week, what you loathed, what you're doing and when you need help. Your leader already knows that. So, they can sit down and have a value-added conversation, and either turn that one-on-one into an hour of, 'How do I help you? How do we focus? How do we keep you playing your strengths?' Or you can turn it into half an hour, and hey, you just cut that time in half, but you're paying positive attention to that employee and helping them be successful.'

Another ritual involves regular engagement pulse surveys through the system. While traditional engagement surveys were deployed every six months or once a year, Cisco teams have a quarterly pulse survey tracked against the eight factors, so that they can keep a finger on how their best teams are being formed and where things are falling off.

By clarifying the behaviours that shape the teams they want, each leader in the organisation has a visible and measurable picture of what they are aspiring to. Through rituals, these behaviours are kept front and centre for each person in the business. While these behaviours are clear and lead from the top, that isn't to say there isn't any flexibility in how these behaviours are adopted as they move down the layers of the business:

> 'In an organisation the size of ours, if you are being clear in setting expectations around behaviour, no matter how clear and confident you are, there will be some adaptation and adoption. There's going to be some localised variance around how much of that gets felt on the ground. There can be a number of mitigating factors, the first line leader being probably the strongest influence of that, of how those behavioural expectations are experienced on the ground.
>
> 'What we need to do is help our leaders interpret those expectations within the bounds of their perception and their experience, characteristics, environment, so that the core elements of conscious culture are felt on the ground with an amount of tolerance for how that plays out in Japan, China, the Netherlands, the US, UK, Australia, New Zealand – understanding that we want the core elements, the core essence of what it means to be part of conscious culture to permeate through the whole organisation, whilst recognising and creating space for adaptation that allows an inclusive experience.'

In Cisco's extensive work around culture, you can see the effort that has gone into making their expectations of each other clear and explicit. These expectations then have a visible and measurable set of behaviours that they seek to replicate in the business, ensuring that people know what 'good' looks like. This set of behaviours are supported by the ongoing rituals and systems, which embed the behaviours as standard practice.

You can't hit a target that you can't see. So, let's paint a bullseye with this conversation.

Having the conversation

Let's put this into practice. While the aim of the first conversation was to move up in the hierarchy of ideas, in this conversation we are looking to 'chunk down' and then 'vote up'. First, we need to make these abstract concepts more specific and concrete, and then we make a decision on which of them matters most.

Much like goal setting, one of the biggest risks of failure is that we allow the conversation to remain too abstract or ambiguous. A good litmus test is to ask this question:

If we all left the room right now, would we know what to do to make this a reality?

To start the conversation, select just one of your core expectations from the first conversation and reflect on some of the following questions.
What would you see and do?

- If you were to leave the room after this conversation and try to spot this in action, what behaviours would you go looking for?
- If you were in a meeting with this team and you noticed us living this out, what would you notice?
- If you were going to encourage a person for living this out, what would you thank them for?
- If you were going to commit to doing one thing that would help us move closer to this, what would you do?

What would you hear or say?

- If you were listening to the way our team talks to one another to identify this in action, what would you be listening for?
- What would you say of this team if you believed we were aligned on this?

To explore what this might look like, let's imagine that one of the core expectations from the first conversation was that the team is connected. As a leader and as a team, it's a quality that you all hold in high regard. But what does it really mean? For some people on your team, being connected might look like spending weekends away together at a holiday house. For others on the team, being connected simply means saying 'Hi' when you arrive at the office. Unless you take the time to chunk down and make the concept less abstract, you run the risk of misinterpretation.

If you take the 'connected' idea down a layer, you might land on something like, 'Our team cares about one another'. Again, this is a great quality, but it's still open to interpretation. Break it down further and you might hear people on your team say something like, 'We take an interest in each other's lives'. In my experience, this is the layer at which many clarifying conversations stop. It may seem like an explicit behaviour, but there is more you can do. Consider it through the lens of what you might see, say, hear and do (as illustrated in Figure 5):

- How would you see someone on your team taking an interest in another person? Maybe you would see people eating lunch together. That is an observable behaviour.
- What would you say that shows you take an interest in other people? If you are asked about someone else on your team, would you be able to talk about more than their job description?
- What would you hear that shows your team taking an interest in each other? Could it be people asking one another about life outside of work, or a conversation about personal interests?
- What might you do to take an interest in another person? Maybe you would attend Friday night drinks rather than leaving work right away, or simply ask about their weekend.

The examples are not exhaustive, but I hope they illustrate the kind of specificity you need to get to in order to make the shared behaviours useful for the people on your team.

Figure 5: Defining behaviours

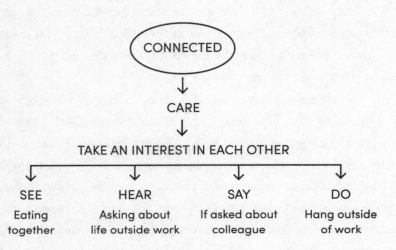

While the core expectations might help people to understand what we value, these can be quickly undermined by our behaviours. For example, we may say that we have an expectation of flexibility and yet be undermined by micromanaging behaviour. We might describe having freedom and autonomy as a core quality of our team and yet measure people by their role output rather than role outcomes.

To take the conversation deeper, you might find it helpful to think about these behaviours through three different lenses:

1. What behaviours are getting in the way of the ideal qualities of our team? These are behaviours to eradicate.
2. What behaviours are we not yet exhibiting that we would like to start doing more often? These are behaviours to establish.

3. What behaviours are we already exemplifying that we would like to prioritise and make a key focus? These are behaviours to enhance.

Take a look at some example behaviours in the table below.

Table 2: Team communication

Eradicate	Establish	Enhance
· Talking about people behind their backs · Refusing to listen to new perspectives · Sharing crude or inappropriate jokes.	· Regularly inviting people to disagree in team meetings · Standing agenda item to give kudos to team mates · Saying 'Hi' to team mates when arriving to work.	· Weekly check-in meetings · Letting each person finish their point before sharing your own · Closing email during meetings.

Share three, pick two

Depending on the size of your team, by the end of this conversation you will likely be standing in front of a wall (or digital board) filled with explicit behaviours that provide a very practical outworking of your shared expectations. There's no real limit on the number, but I generally try to make sure that every person in the room has shared at least three behaviours. This conversation alone can be a powerful team experience to learn more about what each team member values in a very explicit way.

Before you or your team become too overwhelmed looking at all the behaviours, choose which behaviours you want to prioritise. You can't do everything, so you'll need to determine which areas become your core focus.

Don't overcomplicate the process. Here's a simple exercise you can use to find the core behaviours:

1. Give each person two votes. If you're meeting online, you could use a poll. If you're meeting in person, I typically give people two sticky dots.
2. Let the people on your team know that they can place their dot or vote next to just two shared behaviours. Ask each person to select behaviours that are realistic and that they are willing and able to commit to, and which they believe will move the needle closer towards the team culture you all aspire to create.
3. Let people know that they are allowed to vote for one of their own behavioural suggestions, but the second dot must be used on a suggestion from another team member.
4. Once all the votes have been cast, step back and identify the top three clarified behaviours for each of your shared expectations.

As you bring the second conversation to a close, you should have identified a small number of core expectation themes. Beneath each of these themes will be three clarified behavioural expectations of these themes in action.

Once you have these, you're ready for conversation number three.

Action steps

Remember this

- Culture has an observable element.
- The goal of effective communication is to transfer meaning, so take time to clarify meaning – don't interpret it.
- If you can define the culture you want, it will be recognisable when you see it.

- The clarification conversation is about making the invisible observable. Take the time to clarify the observable behaviours that bring your core expectation themes to life.

Try this

Schedule some time with your team to have the clarification conversation. Once you have completed the expectation conversation and have chosen five to seven core themes, you can use these as a guide to 'chunk down' and 'vote up':

- Chunking down the core themes is about reducing ambiguity and producing a set of observable behaviours. You could try asking the following questions:
  - If we all left the room and put this theme into action, what would we see, do, say and hear?
  - If we could commit to two or three behaviours that would help us become more like this, what would they be?
- Take the conversation deeper by reflecting on which behaviours you would like to eradicate, establish or enhance. Encourage each participant to share at least three behaviours.
- Give each person two votes and ask them to vote up the behaviours that they are willing and able to commit to, and that they believe will move the needle closer towards the team culture you aspire to create.
- Agree on the top-priority behaviours based on the team votes, and document them.

Work towards this

By the end of this conversation, each person in your team should be clear about what they can do practically to make these behaviours a reality. You should have a small number of core themes with two or three observable behaviours listed beneath them, something like Figure 6.

Figure 6: Example results of the clarification conversation

Collaboration	Connection	Creativity
Every new project has a clear owner and list of contributors.	We go direct to the person when we have issues.	When a project fails, we meet to discuss learnings.
All meetings have a clear context and agenda.	We ask about people's lives outside of work.	When an idea is presented, we ask questions before making statements.
We don't hold back when we disagree in meetings.	We know the top five strengths of our team.	There is a standing agenda item for sharing learning or ideas.

Chapter 7

The communication conversation

Make the words a language

'Language defines not only the categories of what we see, hear, and feel but how we think about things and define meaning.'
– Edgar H. Schein

Key finding: Only a third of people leaders see shared organisational language as an important ingredient for creating a healthy culture.

Anyone can recite the words, but not everyone can speak the language.

Nigel Richards is widely regarded as one of the greatest tournament Scrabble players of all time. Born and raised in New Zealand, he remains the only player to have become World Champion more than once, having attained the title in 2007, 2011, 2013, 2018 and 2019. While this achievement is impressive, it's his 2015 win at the French World Scrabble Championships that highlights why he is one of the greats. What made this particular win most impressive is that he achieved it without being able to speak French. There were even a number of instances in which he was able to correct his opponent's incorrect choice of words during a match. How did he do it? In preparation for the event, Nigel spent nine weeks studying the French dictionary and committing each word to memory.

And yet, despite knowing every word in the French dictionary, Nigel's victory speech still required him to communicate through an interpreter. Why? Because there is a difference between being able to recite words and the ability to speak the language.

In the expectation conversation, our focus was to identify the words that best describe the culture you have or aspire to create. Those words can provide direction, but they will not create transformation. The words need a shared meaning so that each person can bring them to life. The focus of the clarification conversation was to ensure that each person knows what it looks like to live these expectations out. In the communication conversation, we are going to take this a step further and begin to create a language that empowers the people on your team to talk about these expectations and behaviours consistently so that they become woven into the fabric of your day-to-day conversations.

If you've spent any amount of time at an airport, then it's likely you will have heard the two words nobody likes to hear: 'flight delayed'. It's inconvenient of course, but when it comes to the safety of passengers, it sure beats the alternative.

Having flown with a number of different airlines over the years, one thing has been consistent when I experience a delay: I'm almost guaranteed to hear or overhear the airline crew use the words 'safety over schedule'. When a customer is angry and giving the attendants a piece of their mind, it's this phrase that helps anchor the conversation in the airline's number-one priority: safety. It's this common language that empowers airline crews to speak confidently in moments of inconvenience and disruption.

When we create a set of shared expectations, we give people a common reference point to align around. When we clarify those expectations with a set of shared behaviours that bring meaning, we help create a common understanding and make it actionable. When we create a shared language, we give people a meaningful and memorable way to express and articulate what the team holds in high regard.

Does language really matter?

Sameer B. Srivastava is an Associate Professor at the Haas School of Business at the University of California, Berkeley. Sameer is also a co-director of the Berkeley Culture Initiative, a hub for cutting-edge research on the role of culture in shaping organisational effectiveness and a community of industry leaders and academics who are jointly concerned with, challenged by and excited about organisational culture. I was honoured to have a conversation with him in preparation for this book to learn more about what insights language can teach us about culture. He stressed that while language is not the *only* element of culture, it does provide a valuable window into some of the facets of culture:

> 'I definitely don't think language is everything. How people dress in an organisation tells you something about the culture. How messy their desks are, whether they show up to meetings on time or late. And these are all culturally meaningful signals. I don't mean to privilege language over these other ones. But there are a couple of virtues of thinking about language relative to other measures.
>
> 'What I like about language, and the reason I was drawn to it, is whether people like it or not their cultural style approach leaks out in language.'

Sameer shared with me that one of the reasons language is such a valuable tool for gaining insights into culture, compared with a strictly observational approach such as asking people to complete self-evaluations, is its ability to avoid some of the personal filters and reduce the various reporting biases that occur in these approaches:

'That [approach is] super informative, but very hard to measure at scale and to measure over time. You're constrained by how many ethnographers you can send and where they can go. And what they observe is also coloured a bit by their own filters, what they see. They'll notice some things, but not other things. But it's super valuable. I'm not knocking it. If I knew your interview guide, maybe I would think through bullet points of certain responses, but when you're having a more natural conversation it's very hard to do a lot of... Even politicians giving speeches, parts of their culture will leak out in the course of that speech. So, that's one thing, is that it tells you something about people's identities, about their values, about their beliefs, their assumptions about the world in ways that they can't necessarily massage to fit a particular story.'

When it comes to our interactional language – that is, the language that shows up in our natural conversations (think about the way you communicate over platforms such as Slack, email, Microsoft Teams or Zoom) – he believes this is where we will see language in a much more unselfconscious, automatic and not always deliberate kind of way. The ability we now have through technology to mine large amounts of data means these conversations become easier to measure and analyse. This is exactly what Sameer and his colleagues from Stanford did in their academic paper 'Enculturation Trajectories: Language, Cultural Adaptation, and Individual Outcomes in Organizations'.

In this research project, the team analysed the language within 10.24 million internal emails exchanged over five years among the 601 full-time employees of a mid-sized US for-profit technology firm to better understand how people adapt to organisational culture and what the consequences were for them in the organisation. For example, they looked at how much an employee used swear words when communicating with colleagues who also cursed frequently, or their use of personal pronouns such as 'we' or 'I' to match those used by their peer group. They tracked how an employee would adapt to different cultural conventions of their peers over time.

They found that when there was a high level of cultural fit, it led to more promotions, more favourable performance evaluations, higher bonuses and fewer involuntary departures:

> 'Employees with high cultural fit have a cumulative probability of 48 per cent of being promoted to a managerial position by the end of their third year at the firm, which is 1.5 and 2.7 times greater than their counterparts who exhibit median or low cultural fit, respectively.'

When employees came into the culture and were able to adopt the cultural conventions signified by the language, it was an early predictor of their career trajectory. But there's much more to this research, Sameer told me:

> 'One of the simple analyses we did in one of our papers was to compare the trajectories and subsequent performance of people who came in with high levels of initial cultural fit using our language-based measure, but who exhibited slow learning about the culture.
>
> 'The organisation's culture is not static; every month it's going to look a bit different. People who came in fitting in well

based on language, but then their rate of learning was slow, were compared to the people with the opposite profile (relatively low levels of fit but high adaptability) and the second group significantly outperformed the first. And I think that is perhaps a more general takeaway from that study, that given that culture is adaptive of change and there are various subcultures that exist inside of organisations, and people presumably want to have longer careers – especially the productive ones – and just stick around… screening for adaptability is maybe just as important if not more important than screening for initial fit.'

Many of the conversations I have had with leaders about culture have stressed their concerns about the common notion of hiring for culture fit. Some now prefer to use the language of culture 'add' *or* 'contribution', but what Sameer's research highlights is the important role of cultural adaptability. You need team members who are able to fit within the culture of your team, but more importantly, they also need to be able to adapt with the dynamic nature of culture.

Is language the most important part of shaping a culture by design? No, that's not necessarily the point I'm trying to get across. What Sameer's research illustrates is that language is not something to be ignored. You can learn a lot about the culture of your team by listening to the language in your team. If adaptable employees begin to adopt the language conventions of your team in order to fit in, is it worth considering whether you could be more intentional with it?

Make it meaningful and memorable

In our research, we asked people leaders to share some of the elements that help create a healthy culture, and less than a third told us that 'creating a shared organisational language' was an important ingredient. In my experience, a shared language can be a powerful culture tool in the hand of a leader and their team, but it is often overlooked.

Most of the people leaders we interviewed did not have any mantras, mottos, memes or phrases that helped reinforce cultural expectations within their team. Some of them perhaps spoke about certain topics, such as wellbeing, but they didn't have any phrases that they could recall. Some suggested that the organisational values them-selves could become phrases that were repeated among the team, such as 'Do the right thing' or 'Respect each other', but others felt that 'buzz words' did not help team members understand behavioural expecta-tions and suggested that actions often speak louder than words.

Overall, most leaders I've talked to aren't using language to com-municate cultural expectations or promote shared accountability in their team, and I think they are missing a valuable opportunity.

Let me make one thing very clear: the focus of shared language in your team is empowerment and not control. This is not about telling people how to speak. It's about collaboratively creating language to give expression to the work you've done.

Watch any popular singing show and in each season you will hear a similar critique from the judges: the singer didn't *connect* with the song. What they mean is that the singer was reciting the words, but they didn't connect to a deeper meaning in the song.

To empower the language of your team, the language needs to be both *memorable* and *meaningful*.

When the language of your team is not meaningful or memorable, people will struggle to verbalise what they are working towards with any kind of consistency. They draw on the information they've gained from their own perspectives, and in doing so they develop their own opinions about how the culture should be talked about and articulated, creating even more confusion.

Doing the work to articulate the expectations and behaviours and make sure everyone understands their meaning is deeply important. But when people leave the room and struggle to remember them, or need them attached to an email signature to recall them, then you'll likely end up back in the place of interpretation. When someone asks about the culture and they can't recall what you worked on together, it ends up being talked about inconsistently, resulting in a bunch of hearsay.

Buzz words and jargon occur when we take time to make the language memorable but fail to make it personal or meaningful. The result is clichéd slogans and sayings, which can often have a detrimental outcome. The sayings might be well known in the organisation, but they often come across as insincere and artificial.

I've found that the most effective leaders I know are able to create a shared language with their team that is both meaningful and memorable. These memorable phrases become the mantras and memes that build confidence and belief in the team, and ultimately result in the team feeling deeply empowered (see Figure 7).

Figure 7: Empowering the language of your team

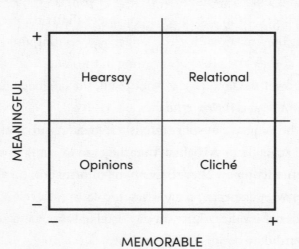

What are memes? You may know 'memes' as a term to describe a funny image on the internet, but memes are much more than that. The word was coined by Richard Dawkins in his book *The Selfish Gene* back in 1976, in which he likened ideas to genes in their ability to evolve and propagate over time:

'Examples of memes are tunes, ideas, catch-phrases, clothes fashions, ways of making pots or of building arches. Just as genes propagate themselves in the gene pool by leaping from body to body via sperm and eggs, so do memes propagate themselves in the meme pool by leaping from brain to brain via a process which, in the broad sense, can be called imitation.'

Think about the shared language – or 'team memes' – as those sticky ideas that have the ability to leap from brain to brain within your team and create a common and empowered way to talk about your culture.

One leader in our interviews shared a simple example of a team meme that effectively created clear behavioural expectations in their organisation and a sense of accountability to these expectations. The phrase was 'TOFU', which stands for 'Take ownership and follow up'. The leader described how this phrase not only created a sense of accountability throughout the organisation but also made it easier to address cultural inconsistencies with colleagues due to its playful nature:

'It's about, "How do we take ownership of our responsibilities within our company and with clients? How do we make sure we are following up?" That became contagious throughout the entire company. If people weren't replying to emails, you would start to get people saying, "You didn't TOFU my request," or "I asked you if you could help me with this project, but you didn't show TOFU," and now we're able to use that acronym as a way to call out those behaviours for people who aren't demonstrating them. Before the acronym, it was a little bit awkward to call someone out and say, "Hey you're lazy". I think TOFU has softened it.'

You can find examples of these cultural memes in a broad range of contexts.

In one of my early leadership roles, we were working hard to change a culture that had been established over a long period of time. In the pre-existing culture, there was a complacency towards work that always ended up at a 'near enough is good enough' outcome. My senior leader at the time introduced a series of memes that he talked about incessantly. The one that is etched in my brain is the phrase 'excellence by choice'. We must have said that phrase a hundred times a day. Over time we noticed people starting to get it. When a job was 80 per cent there and the temptation was to say, 'Close enough', people would ask, 'Is this excellence by choice? Have we done the best we can do here?' I don't want to give full credit to the words here – the words needed actions to underpin them – but it amplified the work we were doing.

Global streaming platform and media services provider Spotify has a clever approach to use of language that can be found on their Life at Spotify webpage, likening the organisation to a band whose members are dependent on each other to create the best audio experience. Tapping into the metaphor of music, they have phrases such as 'No divas' – which is echoed in the words of their CEO Daniel Ek, who says, 'We have no time for entitled egos' – and 'The beat goes on', which means, 'When we win, we celebrate the success together. When we fail, we celebrate the new valuable information that we learned. Failure is an important part of our process'.

When Google was just a few years old, they wrote what is known as their 'Ten things we know to be true', a list they continue to revisit that gives some great examples of shared language embedded into the philosophy of how they work. 'You don't need to be at your desk to need an answer' speaks to the increasingly mobile nature of society and the work they are doing to make technology that supports people on the go. 'You can be serious without a suit' reminds people that while the atmosphere might be casual, they take work seriously and move at a fast pace.

A few years ago, I was coaching an executive who was leading her team through the rollout of a new strategic plan. While some areas of the strategy required strict execution, many aspects of the plan allowed her team the freedom and flexibility to innovate and explore new possibilities for achieving outcomes.

Her primary challenge was to make it easy for the team to differentiate between the two. As with many great challenges, communication was the answer. When I asked about her personal interests, she told me she loved music. We ran with the metaphor and empowered the team to ask a simple question when it came to the strategy: 'Is this orchestral, or is this jazz?'

In an orchestra, you play to the sheet music you're given. In jazz, the melody is set and then musicians take turns to improvise and explore. Some aspects of the strategy were orchestral – you play what's on the paper. Other aspects of the strategy were jazz – you improvise and explore within boundaries. This phrase gave people on the team a common language to help make sense of what was required of them in that moment.

This is the power of language.

Neither you nor I are naive enough to believe that a meme or phrase will always reflect the current reality of your culture, but it will give people a glimpse into what you aspire to be. It will provide people with a common language that empowers them to articulate the culture you have and are working together to build.

Make it personal and relatable

Stories bring the language to life. Stories can help people connect with and embed your cultural language and core expectations by making them personal and relatable.

Gabrielle Dolan (aka Ral) is a bestselling author and Australia's foremost thought leader on business storytelling. She is regarded around the world for her expertise in bringing humanity to the way businesspeople communicate. When I sat down with her for a conversation about the importance of storytelling, she told me:

'You cannot communicate values through bullet points, and you cannot communicate cultural change just through logic. The vast majority of the work I do is going in and helping leaders bring their values to life through the leaders sharing personal stories.

'I think where cultural change goes wrong is that we spend a lot of time coming up with our purpose and our values and our mission and not a lot of time getting our people leaders to connect with it on a really personal level.

'Every individual people leader needs to go through the process of saying, "Well, what does that mean to me personally?" When I ask them, they give me a very corporate response and I go, "Okay, but what else does it mean? Thinking personally, what else does it mean?" And after about 20 seconds, the vast majority of people will say, "Gee, you've really put me on the spot here. I haven't thought about it this much before". And they haven't.

'I truly, truly, truly believe that without sharing stories around your company values, the words will be words on a wall, and they'll stay words on a wall.'

In her book *Real Communication: How to Be You and Lead True*, Ral published this story of Anne Bennett, which illustrates this idea brilliantly. I reached out to Anne, who gave me permission to share it here.

'My dad was a professional swimmer when he was young. At sixteen years old he was in the backstroke finals to make it into the 1964 Tokyo Olympic Games team for Australia. Dad flew out of the blocks and was out in front of all his competitors but as he approached his turn at the 50 metres, he missed the wall. Knowing he hadn't made the touch, he swam back, touched the wall and kept racing. Dad came in seventh that day and missed out on making the Olympic squad. After finishing, the judges told him that they hadn't seen the missed touch (it was well before technology recorded this). If he had kept going, he would have come first and broken a world record. Dad would always tell my sister and me that he has never regretted that split-moment decision. Even though the judges didn't see the missed touch, he knew he had missed it and he knew it was the right thing to do. For me doing the right thing is a lifelong lesson shown to me by my dad and the integrity he showed that day. When I think of integrity I think of my dad. We will often be faced with situations in business where we have to decide if we go back and touch the wall or not. It is at these times I always ask myself what my dad would do.'

A story like this brings the word 'integrity' alive. It's not just memorable and meaningful, it's also personal and relatable. It's not just a word printed on the wall or written in a document – it comes alive in the story.

According to Ral, what makes Anne's story such a great example is the impact it had on the behaviours in the team. She shared how

'This is our go-back-and-touch-the-wall moment' became a common phrase to ensure decisions were made through the lens of integrity. It became a team meme.

Stories can help shape your culture, and you can learn a lot about your culture by the stories that are shared. Ral put it perfectly when she told me:

'I could go sit in the foyer or sit in the tearoom and can tell a culture by the stories I'm hearing, or overhearing there... When the stories are changing, the culture is changing.'

You don't need an Olympic story to bring your culture to life – you have your own. Your team is full of valuable stories waiting to be told.

Isn't this just jargon?

There's a lot to be said around organisational jargon. It cops a bad rap from commentators. And yet in our research, when we asked people leaders what contributed to unhealthy culture, less than one in four cited organisational jargon.

Anne Curzan, in an interview on the *HBR IdeaCast* podcast episode 'Why Business Jargon Isn't All Bad', shared that there are some upsides to having organisational jargon.

Having language in common can actually create helpful shortcuts for talking about expectations of each other and helping people feel more like insiders. The danger is that unhelpful jargon can have the opposite effect and create environments where people feel excluded from the team.

'TOFU' is a helpful acronym when the story accompanies it. The 'touch-the-wall moment' is meaningful when we understand why touching the wall matters. When it comes to creating your common language, just remember to include others in the shared meaning.

Having the conversation

Let's bring this all together. For this conversation, you will work through the list of your core expectations with the clarified behaviours. At this point in the process, you will have identified some of the most meaningful expectations to you and your team. Beneath those core themes, you will have a small number of clarified behaviours that make it very clear what this expectation looks like in practice. In this conversation, you will be mining for everyday language, memes and stories to help bring these expectations to life for your team.

You might find it helpful to think of this conversation in two parts: sharing stories and refining language.

Share stories – what does this mean to you personally?

A great way to start this conversation is to encourage your team to find their own personal stories that bring the expectations and behaviours to life. Be careful not to rush this part of the process. This isn't just a great opportunity to identify some common language, it's also a deeply enriching experience to listen to the stories of people on your team. We spend so much time working alongside each other, but often we know very little about each other outside of work. The stories each person shares can tell you a little more about what they like, what they value, what lights them up, what they have had to navigate or overcome and what they bring to the team.

Pick one of the core themes or behaviours and ask people to share the following:

- What personal stories to come to mind when you hear this word?
- When have you (or someone you know) done this well?
- When have you (or someone you know) failed at this?
- Who is someone that embodies this?
- What experience taught you this the hard way?

Many people who I've had the opportunity to work with on storytelling will push back on sharing their personal stories, for a couple of reasons. First, they feel like they don't have any stories to tell (they always do). As a leader, you need to be ready to ask questions that elicit stories. Ask open questions that cannot be answered with a 'yes' or 'no' response. Probe for examples that draw out stories from people.

Second, people often say that their story feels self-indulgent to share, or that nobody would care about their stories. This couldn't be further from the truth.

A simple framework I walk leaders through is to consider their story through the lens of the past, present and future:

- **Past:** Reflect on what happened. What is the necessary information required in order for you to communicate the essence of this story? Keep it to around 60 to 90 seconds.
- **Present:** Reflect on your learning. What was that experience all about? As you put it under the microscope with the gift of hindsight, what big learning can you draw from the story? What themes exist in this story?
- **Future:** Reflect on the connection. How does the learning from this story connect to the core expectations or behaviours you're trying to promote in your culture? What are some of the key phrases or memes that showed up in the story that people could apply in their own context?

Go back and read Anne's story. It might be about the 1964 Tokyo Olympics, but it's not about the Olympics. It was a lesson from her dad about doing the right thing. That lesson becomes helpful to others by bringing their value of integrity to life.

Stories are a vehicle. They serve a purpose. If everybody remembers the story but forgets the message, then everybody has missed the point. What helps a story feel less self-indulgent is when a story is shared in service of others. That's why it's always so important to ensure the connection between the story and the reason for sharing the story is made clear. Ral calls this the 'bridge'.

As you listen to the stories, it would be helpful to find a way to capture them so they can be remembered and shared.

Refine language – how would you talk about this normally?

As you reflect on the stories, listen closely for the messaging that begins to emerge. It could be a phrase or a few words. Memes could be a song lyric, a sound or an expression. For Anne's story it was the phrase 'touch the wall'. These phrases can help you to refine the language you choose to make your cultural expectations and behaviours part of your everyday vocabulary.

As you work with your team to refine some of your internal team memes, you could reflect on some of these questions:

- What phrases come to mind that relate to this expectation or behaviour?
- What metaphors does this make me think of?
- What song lyrics do I hear in my head?
- What is something I always hear said?
- What is the best piece of advice I've been given in this area?
- Reflect on your hobbies or interests and consider whether there are any expressions used that might apply here.

Maybe you will end up with a metaphor like Spotify's 'No divas' that helps refine your memes. I worked with a team who used the Kenny Rogers lyrics 'know when to hold 'em, know when to fold 'em' as a way to talk about when a person was digging their heels in and being stubborn in a meeting.

Netflix uses the phrase 'fight the python of process' to talk about their culture of freedom, and Amazon has the phrase 'have a backbone; disagree and commit' embedded into their leadership principles to invite diverse thinking but maintain alignment.

You don't have to reinvent the wheel. Are there already great expressions you could adapt into your team vocabulary that best articulate your core themes? Organisational theorist Karl Wieck has a great expression that I've heard embedded as a team meme to point to expectations around collaboration and respect: 'Fight as if you're right. Listen as if you're wrong'. When I wrote *Lead the Room*, I introduced a phrase about simplifying your message that I share with everyone I work with: 'Start with clarity – end with simplicity'.

Your phrases or team memes should be clear in their purpose and simple in their language. Leadership author and speaker Andy Stanley is known for his phrase 'Memorable is portable', meaning that when people can remember it, they can take it and use it.

If you want them to be easy to remember and hard to forget, consider the following:

- Is it possible to write this phrase more simply?
- Does this phrase communicate the point clearly?
- Will we use these words or phrases naturally?
- Can I and the team recall these phrases easily?

Take time with your team to refine the language so that each phrase is not just memorable but rich with meaning.

By the end of this conversation, you should have a number of phrases or team memes that you and your team can start to incorporate into your daily working to help each person talk about your shared expectations and behaviours. You should also have a number of stories to share that help people connect personally and meaningfully to your culture.

Before we explore conversations four and five, we need to find a way to capture what we have achieved so far. We'll explore this in the next chapter.

Action steps

Remember this

- The communication conversation is about making the words a language. While words can provide valuable direction, they will not create transformation alone.
- A shared language is about empowering the people on your team to talk about expectations and behaviours consistently, so they become woven into the fabric of your day-to-day conversations.
- Language is for empowerment, not control.
- When language is meaningful but not memorable, people resort to hearsay. When language is memorable but not meaningful, people resort to clichés. In the absence of both, they rely on opinion.
- 'Team memes' are sticky ideas that have the ability to leap from brain to brain within your team and create a common and empowered way to talk about your culture. They result from language that is both memorable and meaningful.
- Stories help bring cultural language to life.

Try this

Schedule some time with your team to have the communication conversation. Look at your core theme expectations and their list of clarified behaviours. 'Mine for memes' by exploring language and stories:

- As a leader, sharing your own story first can help set the tone for the vulnerability of the stories that will be told. The psychological safety that exists will also limit or enhance the vulnerability of the stories shared.

- To find stories, try asking the following questions:
  - What personal stories come to mind when you see these words?
  - Who do you know who embodies this, and why?
  - What experience taught you this the hard way?
- When sharing stories, home in on the language or phrases used and try to find your 'go back and touch the wall' moments.
- To find key language or phrases, try asking the following questions:
  - What phrases come to mind that relate to these expectations or behaviours?
  - What metaphors, song lyrics or memorable quotes does this make me think of?
- Once you have some of the phrases collected, consider the following questions for each one:
  - How could we simplify this statement?
  - How would we use this phrase in everyday language?
  - How can we make this memorable?

Work towards this

By the end of this conversation, you will have a number of phrases – or 'team memes' – that you and your team can start to incorporate into your daily work to help each person talk about your shared expectations and behaviours. You will also have several stories to share that help people connect personally and meaningfully to your culture, and which will help in communicating that culture to others. It should look something like Figure 8.

Figure 8: Example results of the communication conversation

Collaboration	Connection	Creativity
Every new project has a clear owner and list of contributors.	We go direct to the person when we have issues.	When a project fails, we meet to discuss learnings.
All meetings have a clear context and agenda.	We ask about people's lives outside of work.	When an idea is presented, we ask questions before making statements.
We don't hold back when we disagree in meetings.	We know the top five strengths of our team.	There is a standing agenda item for sharing learning or ideas.
Disagree and commit.	Talk to, not about.	Be curious, not judgmental.
Story: 'Coaching son's soccer team'	Story: 'Voicemail – leave a message you're proud of'	Story: 'Gardening – beautiful things grow through the dirt'

Chapter 8

Pick three and make it easy to see

Focus on what matters most

'Basically, the more you try to do, the less you actually accomplish. This is a stark, inescapable principle we all live with. Somewhere along the way, most leaders forget this.'
– Sean Covey, Jim Huling and Chris McChesney

Key finding: Most people leaders (84%) believe that creating a healthy culture with their team is the most important part – or one of the most important parts – of their role.

When everything is a priority, is anything a priority?

Speaking the language of Gallup's CliftonStrengths, I lead with my dynamic duo of ideation and belief. This means that when I'm presented with the opportunity to connect the dots in a new and creative way on something I'm passionate about, it's not uncommon for me to drop everything in pursuit of that new idea.

I've learned the hard way what I'm sure you're already well aware of: you can't do everything – at least, not well.

It seems counterintuitive that the path to better is to do less, when for most of our careers we are rewarded (and even promoted) because of our ability to do more. As a leader, that pursuit of more is a dangerously alluring way to prove your worth.

Don't mistake doing less for putting in less effort. It's about investing that effort with the right focus. The light from a lamp might illuminate a room, but the light from a laser can cut through steel – that's the power of focus. If you're not clear on what matters most, it's easy to get caught up in what matters now. Focusing on less will ultimately help you and your team to achieve more. This is true of your strategy and your work, and it's also true of your culture. Your team needs clear priorities when it comes to building the culture you want.

Of course, you can do it all eventually – you just don't need to do it all right now.

At the end of our first three conversations – and we still have two to go – you will have identified a set of core expectation themes. They empower your team to have meaningful conversations about what you are working towards and what aligns you. From these expectations, you will have classified a core set of behaviours that your team agrees will move you in the direction of that expectation. Finally, you will have created some team memes, phrases, language and stories to help bring the expectations and behaviours to life.

As Sheryl Sandberg says, it's time for 'ruthless prioritisation':

'I think [it's] the most important thing we've learned as we've grown… only do the very best of the ideas. Lots of times you have very good ideas. But they're not as good as the most important thing you could be doing. And you have to make the hard choices.'

The $100 game

I was first introduced to the $100 game by my friend Alicia McKay, a leadership, strategy and change expert, while we were speaking together at an event in Sydney. The $100 game (or the $100 test) is commonly used in software development for working with users to create a prioritised feature list. However, it can be applied in a broad range of contexts in which participants need to create a sense of false scarcity. Alicia unpacks the rules of the $100 game in her book *From Strategy to Action: A Guide to Getting Shit Done in the Public Sector*:

> 'The premise of the $100 game is to assess the relative priority of your high-priority issues. The rules of the game are as follows: You only have $100 to spend. This represents the finite amount of energy, bandwidth and attention (not to mention resources) available to you. You cannot divide the $100 perfectly equally, i.e. $33 across three, or $25 across four. If you award something $10 or less, consider removing it. Interestingly, something usually (but not always) receives $50 or more.'

As you and your team take a step back and look at the list of core expectations and clarified behaviours, how would you spend your $100? What does this exercise reveal to you about what your top priorities are for the culture you want?

Hopefully this stage of the process will leave you with a clear indication of your top priorities. You might find that the $100 game doesn't let you have more than three main priorities. Spoiler: that's the point. Not everything can be a priority right now.

Don't discard the remaining work. Just because these things are not your top priority does not mean they are irrelevant. Culture is dynamic, and what matters now may change. The work you have done to get to this point is important and valuable.

In an interview for *The 4 Disciplines of Execution*, Tim Tassopoulos, who is the President and COO of Chick-Fil-A, said, 'The first thing I want to know when I am talking to a leader is, where has that leader chosen to spend disproportionate energy?' This game is about learning where to apply disproportionate energy right now. The third discipline of execution in this book is to 'keep a compelling scoreboard… to make sure everyone knows the score at all times, so that they can tell whether or not they are winning'. We have not done all this hard work for something to be out of sight and out of mind.

Make it easy to see

James Clear has become widely known for his expertise in building better personal habits, particularly off the back of his bestselling book *Atomic Habits*, in which he discusses his four laws of behaviour change. James's first law is to make the new behaviour obvious and more visible. He uses the example of placing vitamins on top of the refrigerator as a visual cue to take his vitamins when going to eat, or buying a new water bottle to have at your desk as a reminder to drink more water. The power of a visual cue cannot be underestimated.

Is the next step to print out culture cards and stick them to each team member's desk, or start printing glossy posters for your wall? I hope not, but if that works for you, then all power to you. However, I do think there is something to be said about making your cultural aspirations visible, front of mind and easy to see for the people on your team and for new members who join your team.

Aurecon is an Australian design, engineering and advisory company that brings ideas to life to create a better future for people and the planet. I was first introduced to their work while speaking at a conference alongside Danielle Bond, Group Director, Brand, Marketing & Communications. In 2018 Aurecon launched Australia's first visual employment contract. Yes, that is exactly as it sounds. Their team was able to 'eliminate more than 4000 words from their employment contracts to create a succinct and meaningful visual contract that uses illustrations to complement the text'. This idea was deeply aligned to their DNA and guiding principles, one of which is to 'make the complex simple'.

Aurecon's visual contract is a great example of finding new ways to make something visible. In addition to their visual contract, they have also created something they call their 'Aurecon Attributes': a collection of qualities they believe make them who they are. Employees are given the opportunity to take a short assessment to find their standout attributes, and are given a coffee cup to take to meetings that makes those attributes visible to others on their team. This helps each team member appreciate the contribution of each other person in the room and recognise when they are lacking certain qualities needed to bring out the best in the discussion. Something as simple as a coffee cup can help create a powerful visual cue.

Another great example of this was that, as lockdowns were lifting across Australia, Corrie and the team at Thendro created wristbands for their staff and customers with the abbreviation 'DBAD' written on them. It stood for 'Don't Be A Dick', a phrase she told me had become popular among their team. As people were being rude and suffering from mental health issues, it was a way of telling customers and staff to be kind. These wristbands were a visual cue to remind people of their values of being forthright while staying open and accepting.

Capturing what you have discussed doesn't need a large amount of money or resources. It could be as simple as creating a brief PowerPoint slide deck to record your shared expectations, behaviours and language, and having that readily available and accessible for your team to go back and refer to. You could use your smartphone and ask each team member to capture on video some of their stories that bring these themes to life. I know of one client who bought each of her staff members a desk plant as a visual cue of their culture of 'Growth requires change'. There are so many ways you can make your culture visible; the key is finding ways to keep the work you've done front of mind for you and your team.

Sameer Srivastava shared with me a simple but powerful ritual used in the faculty meetings of the Haas School of Business when they were trying to get academics to become more attuned to the issues of diversity, equity and inclusion:

> 'So, we engage with research. The question was how best to do that. And one of our associate deans had a brilliant idea that we would start faculty meetings with a five-minute to seven-minute summary of a research paper that was about diversity, equity and inclusion.
>
> 'In our case, it was less about giving people a playbook of language but giving people a research finding, and you can just take five minutes to discuss and debate how much you believe it and what you think it needs.
>
> 'It became a ritual. Every meeting started this way for a good two years until I think people started to kind of shift a bit and say, "This is not just some throwaway topic. This is something that we all need to make a top priority".'

What rituals can you and your team create that help make your cultural priorities more visible? Could you create a standing agenda item at the beginning of your team meeting to talk about your culture journey?

Is there a behaviour that you and your team have agreed is important that you could create a ritual around? I heard a great example from a senior HR leader in the not-for-profit sector who wanted to shape a stronger culture of celebration in the business for people who were arriving and also for those who were leaving. They created a ritual they described as the airport lounge. It was a monthly morning tea at which new team members were welcomed into the business and departing team members were honoured for their service to the business. They played on the metaphor of an airport as a place where new arrivals are met with a sense of joy and excitement and farewelled with a sense of sadness but well-wishing for their journey ahead.

Averages and aspirations

I once heard someone say that culture isn't just what is written on the wall, it's everything that is taking place down the hall. Culture is about averages, not aspirations. You can all agree that on your team you have a culture of inclusion, but you might operate in a way that is in direct conflict. You could say you have a culture of empowerment and yet micromanage each employee to death. Culture is the shared norms of your team, not the shared aspirations. But that isn't to say culture can't be aspirational.

The conversations we have had so far in this journey will more than likely reflect aspects of your culture that are strong and those that need to develop. What matters is that you and your team are committed to making progress towards becoming the team you want.

How do you measure the invisible? We know that in many ways culture is this invisible and intangible quality, which makes measuring progress challenging. We know from our research that people leaders are looking for ways to assess whether culture is changing in a healthy or an unhealthy way, and for tools to measure whether they are achieving their cultural strategy.

Don't overcomplicate it right now. There are a number of organisational assessments that you could undertake to measure different aspects of your culture, which have value. But here's what you can do right now. Take a moment with your team to look through and reflect on your prioritised list of cultural expectations and behaviours. Ask your team members to consider on a scale of one to ten how much these reflect the current reality of your team, with one being 'This doesn't reflect us at all' and ten being 'This perfectly describes our team'. Ask each person to write their score for each of the core expectations anonymously and without discussion. Pick the first expectation and add up the total score from your team, then divide it by the number of people who voted to get the average score. For example, if the scores given were 4, 6, 3, 6, 4, 5 and 3, you would divide the total of 31 by 7, giving you an average score of 4.4 out of 10.

My wife has spent most of her career in the field of human resources. When it comes to conducting their employee engagement scores, she has a common phrase she shares: 'There are no bad scores. The only bad scores are those which we do nothing about'.

When you're looking at your culture score, you might be pleasantly surprised, or you might want to crawl into a hole. Don't let a high score go to your head, and don't let a low score deflate you. The score just reflects a moment in time – what you do with it is what matters most. You can do this exercise on a regular basis and track your collective effort.

As you monitor the culture score over time, you simply want to know that the efforts invested by you and your team are moving the needle in the direction of becoming the team you want. How can you make that scorecard more visible so people know whether or not they are winning?

Whether the score is moving in a positive or negative direction, take time as a team to reflect on what specifically has caused it. What do you need to stop, start or continue doing to keep making progress?

Action steps

Remember this

- When everything is a priority, nothing is a priority. You can't do it all – at least, not at the same time.
- Your team needs clear priorities when it comes to building the culture you want.
- Prioritising doesn't mean putting in less effort. It's about investing that effort with the right focus.
- Choose the areas you want to apply disproportionate energy to right now that will help create the team culture you want.
- Make the priorities visible to yourself and your team through items, visuals or rituals.
- Culture is about averages not aspirations, but culture can be aspirational.

Try this

- Take time with your team to explore the list of core expectation themes, clarified behaviours and shared language.
- Consider the following questions:
  - Which of these areas should we apply disproportionate energy to?
  - If we could just pick three to focus on right now, which would help us create the culture we want?
- Use the $100 game to help you and your team narrow down your top priorities.
- Brainstorm some ideas to help make these priorities visible to the team.
- Once you have picked your top three priorities, take a moment to evaluate where you are now in relation to your aspirations in each area. Team members can use a simple one-to-ten scale to vote.

The average score is your initial benchmark, which you can use to regularly evaluate your progress against.

· Set a regular cadence for evaluating progress.

Work towards this

The team has three cultural aspirations and priorities to start working towards. Each has a set of clarified behaviours, along with some language to help communicate those behaviours.

PART THREE
KEEPING THE
CONVERSATION
GOING

In July 2020, 60 eager passengers showed up to Taipei Songshan Airport with their boarding passes in hand, ready to take a trip. At the height of a global pandemic, with borders locked down, you might find yourself wondering where they were going. The answer? Nowhere. With flights grounded because of COVID-19, Taipei Songshan Airport offered locals who were missing travel the chance to get a small taste in their 'pretend to go abroad' tour.

Ting Hsu, who works in the airport's planning department, told *CNN Travel*, 'In addition to letting the participants go through security screening, identification inspection and other immigration clearance procedures, they actually boarded the plane to experience the fun of boarding'.

Somewhere, someone had thought to themselves, 'How can we get people to pay for all the frustrations of travel without any of the benefits?'

When I work with my clients to facilitate their culture conversations, they are always so proud of what they've been able to accomplish thus far. If you've had the conversations, you should be able to look at some kind of document that paints a picture of the culture you aspire to have. But the work on shaping a culture by design doesn't end when you're all clear on the team you want – it's really just beginning. If you stop here, you're on a plane going nowhere. You've put in all the effort of going through airport security just to sit on the tarmac. If you file it away and never speak of it again, then it will just become another conversation that didn't eventuate to anything meaningful. You can change that.

What we know about culture is that there is an element that is collective in nature. It requires the buy-in of everybody to become the norms of the group. Social learning also plays an important role in shaping that collective experience. We take notice of what is rewarded and what is punished in the group to help us shape these norms. We look to role models to help show the way.

If you think back to the way you learned what was acceptable and unacceptable in your house growing up, you'll find that it was shaped in a few ways. First, by watching your role models. What did they do, and what was the outcome? What did your older sibling do, and did they get away with it? Second, we learned through experiencing which behaviours were celebrated and which were confronted. You likely learned the importance of saying 'Thank you' by being reprimanded when you forgot or encouraged when you did it without being asked.

It sounds like classic behavioural conditioning. You know Ivan Pavlov's ringing bell and salivating dog? But there's a difference. We're not just trying to get people to mindlessly start or stop a behaviour. We need to help people understand why. It's intentional.

When it comes to the ongoing conversations around shaping culture, we need to strike the balance between the good and the bad. We need to be willing to confront counter-cultural behaviours when we see them, and just as importantly, we need to reward the behaviours that shape the culture we want.

In Part Three of this book, we're going to explore the final two conversations that help shape a shared accountability and the way we can keep the culture conversations alive. You'll notice that the framework for these is directed towards you as the leader. Don't assume this narrow focus means these conversations only go in one direction. It's just as crucial for your team to be able to have these conversations with you.

These are the final two conversations:

1. **Confronting conversations:** These conversations challenge and redirect the behaviours that do not align with the shared expectations of the team. When we choose not to have these conversations, we can be unintentionally reinforcing these behaviours and allowing them to continue.
2. **Confirming conversations:** These conversations confirm and reward the culture-building behaviours that align with our shared expectations. When we have these conversations, we encourage the repetition of the core behaviours that shape the culture we want.

Like many things in the workplace, the frequency of each type of conversation will involve a delicate tension to manage. If we only ever confront counter-culture behaviour, we end up with a whole lot of depressed people. Your team members will end up walking around waiting for someone to jump on their faults. They will operate from a place that believes, 'I'm no good'. They'll end up thinking they 'can't do anything right'.

If we only ever confirm good behaviour, we end up with a team full of deluded people. I think about it as being like the singing show contestant who has been told their entire life they are a great singer, only to face the harsh reality of the judges and public. These people walk around waiting for affirmation for the work they do. They operate from the belief, 'I'm so good'. They'll end up thinking they 'can't do anything wrong'.

I close out Part Three (and the book) by looking at how culture can go too far and what we can do to avoid this, and then wrap up with some closing thoughts on where to start and what to do next.

Chapter 9

The confrontation conversation

Make feedback less difficult

'The culture of any organization is shaped by the worst
behavior the leader is willing to tolerate.'
– Steve Gruenert and Todd Whitaker

Key finding: Just one third of people leaders feel
empowered to speak up when they see a culture and
values misalignment.

---

*There he is, seated across the table from me, completely oblivious
to the fact that he's just shut me down in front of everybody else
in the meeting. He almost certainly did it on purpose. Here I am,
wishing the ground would swallow me whole, and he doesn't
even seem concerned. I thought this team valued innovation
and diverse perspectives? The meeting finally ends and I see him
making a dash for the door, so I rush to pull him aside to tell him
that what he did was not OK.*

The conversation begins calmly but it quickly escalates. We're like two sword fighters exchanging powerful blows back and forth. He raises his voice, and I raise mine. I call him out on his behaviour, and he deflects it back towards me as though I'm overreacting. Before long we're both losing control of our emotions, words start flying out of our mouths, and we start saying things we both wish we could take back.

Suddenly I snap back to reality as the manager calls for my attention in the room.

Have you ever had one of those arguments with a colleague in your mind? I've lost count of how many I've had, personally – you know, that mental back and forth in your mind when you're staring down the barrel of a difficult conversation. I'm prone to imagining them through the worst possible scenario, one that almost never occurs.

It's just one conversation. It's not a big deal, right? The pit in your stomach when you cross paths with that person would suggest otherwise.

VitalSmarts, an organisation you may know for their work on 'Crucial Conversations', found that employees waste an average of $1500 and an eight-hour workday for every crucial conversation they avoid.

But who really *enjoys* having a difficult conversation?

The hard truth about cultural inconsistencies, though, is that if you won't confront them, you can't change them, and if you can't change them, you'll struggle to create the team you want. In our interviews with people leaders, one participant put it this way:

'I feel like people can have the perspective that culture just happens and that you can't influence it, and I feel that those cultures often can end up toxic because bad habits start to get ingrained in the culture. People start accepting things that are unhealthy as the norm and that then becomes the culture. There's really no framework for what we do and don't tolerate.'

There's an old proverb that says, 'No news is good news'. As it turns out, no news is actually very bad news for employees.

According to Gallup, you're about twice as likely to be actively disengaged at work when your manager ignores you compared to if they focus on your weaknesses or negative characteristics. They also found that employees who strongly agreed that they had received 'meaningful feedback' in the past week were almost four times more likely than other employees to be engaged at work.

Silence is a breeding ground for ambiguity. People need clarity. They want to know where they stand. Don't carry the weight of a frustration that could be resolved by an effective conversation.

Liane Davey put it well when we she said, 'Carrying an issue without resolution is like carrying debt. You'll eventually have to pay the principal (by having the difficult conversation), but the longer you wait, the more interest you'll pay in anxiety and dread'.

I have never found it easy to deliver tough feedback, but I've found that having a framework and some practice can make the conversation feel less difficult and more empowering. We're going to break down the confrontation conversation into a practical step-by-step process you can follow to make these confronting conversations a little easier.

You might find it helpful to think about this conversation in three parts: think through, talk through and follow through (see Figure 9). Respectively, these parts link to the process you can follow leading up to the conversation, during the conversation and after the conversation.

Figure 9: (Less) 'difficult' conversations

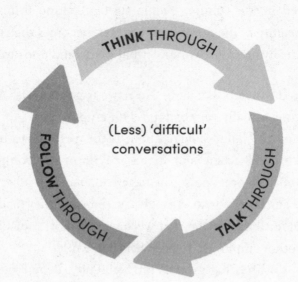

THINK THROUGH

(Less) 'difficult'
conversations

TALK THROUGH

FOLLOW THROUGH

Think through

Feedback conversations are less difficult when you take the time to intentionally think them through. One of the biggest mistakes we can make heading into a confronting conversation is to go in carelessly. Many people I talk to who have had a bad experience with a difficult conversation didn't have an issue because the person they were talking to was malicious – although there are those examples – but rather because the person hadn't fully thought through the situation.

Hanlon's Razor states, 'Never attribute to malice that which can be adequately explained by stupidity'. Many hard conversations I've experienced were not ill-intended, just poorly thought through. If you commit to thoroughly thinking, not only are you better prepared for the conversation, but you may find you don't need to have the conversation at all. So, what should you think through?

Purpose

Why are you having this conversation? It's important to consider whether this is a conversation that needs to happen at all. Is this an issue of performance or just a clash of preferences? Is this getting in the way of your collective success, or is it simply a difference in personality? Your shared expectations and behaviours are an invaluable tool to help you see the purpose of the conversation through the lens of the culture you are trying to create.

Outcome

Is this a problem or a complaint? What distinguishes a problem from a complaint is an outcome or solution. What would you like to look different by the end of this conversation? What is this person doing (or not doing) right now that you would like them to stop (or start) after the meeting? The answer to this question needs to be concrete, not abstract. A simple way to make this more specific is to think about what you might notice if this behaviour changes.

Support

What support might this person need to make the change you're asking of them? Do you have the budget, resources or network to assist this person to follow through on what they have been asked to do? If the person asks for training or coaching, is this an option? Will this person need an additional support person during the conversation?

Temperature

Is this conversation hot or cold? This is a concept I was first introduced to by Mark Gerzon in his 2014 *Harvard Business Review* article, 'To Resolve a Conflict, First Decide: Is It Hot or Cold?' He explained: 'Hot conflict is when one or more parties are highly emotional...

Cold conflict is when one or more parties seem to be suppressing emotions, or actually appear "unemotional".

When thinking through the conversation, you will need to consider how the person typically responds to conflict and think through how you might deal with conflict that gets hot or cold. If the conversation gets heated, you might like to press pause and take some time to let it cool down. If the conversation is cold, you might want to start more personally to warm things up.

Timing

When is the right time to have this conversation? Is this a conversation that can happen at the end of a meeting, or does it need a more formalised invitation? Be sure to address misaligned behaviours quickly. Don't wait – gather evidence and build your case. By having the conversation early, you can pre-empt bigger conversations down the road and prevent small behaviours from becoming habits.

Considering the timing of the conversation will also determine where and how the conversation will take place. Is this going to be face to face or virtual? How does the environment affect your ability to communicate openly? A friend of mine shared an experience in her multi-level office building where the glass on the meeting rooms was not frosted and looked out onto open-plan working space. Whenever a difficult conversation needed to happen, people were taken to a different level to ensure nobody on their team could see the conversation taking place. However, people quickly learned that when a meeting was scheduled on a different floor, it was not likely to be a great conversation.

Plan

Once you have taken the time to think the conversation through, you should have a plan that outlines why the conversation is important, what the problem is, what needs to change and how you can support the person to make that change. Take a moment to write down your most accessible next step from there to set up the conversation.

Talk through

Feedback conversations are much less difficult when you go in with a plan. Having a process to follow can help you locate yourself in the conversation and provide you with a practical next step to guide the path forward. Some people I talk to feel restricted by a process. They say it can end up feeling a little robotic. I can understand that. Any process will feel a little clunky as you start out. Over time, though, you learn to adapt the language and find a flow that works best for you. Eventually the process will become much more automatic for you. For now, trust the process, because it works.

Once you have taken time to set the context for the conversation, think through these six key moments in the conversation.

Observation

Start by making an observation from your perspective. What behaviour did you notice that warranted this conversation? It's important for you to make the behaviour explicit and ensure you are able to give the person practical examples of this behaviour in action. While empathy plays an important role in this conversation, at this point it's important to remove the emotion from the observation. Speak directly about what you could see or observe rather than about how it made you feel.

For example: 'I noticed during our last meeting you were looking down on your laptop for a large portion of the meeting and didn't contribute much to the conversation we were having as a team'.

Impact

What was the felt impact of this behaviour for you or your team? What was the consequence of their behaviour that could have been avoided? The purpose of this conversation is to address cultural inconsistencies in order to build and shape culture, so at this point it's important that you clearly make the connection between the exhibited behaviours of the team member and the shared expectations and clarified behaviours you created in the previous conversations. For example: 'When you were on your laptop, the team and I didn't get to hear any of your ideas or contribution to the conversation. We all agreed that as a team we wanted to create a culture of collaboration, which means contributing to the conversation in our meetings, and that didn't happen today'.

Input

This is the one stage in the process that can change everything. When addressing cultural inconsistencies, it's important to remember that you are looking at one side of the die – you are missing the complete picture. I personally choose to enter each conversation hoping to be wrong. I want to hear a side of the story that changes my perspective. That doesn't always happen, but I need to be humble enough to recognise I could be wrong. So, before going any further, ask them for their input. Try asking, 'What do you think about that?'

What if their response is, 'I'm so sorry, I know I was distracted in that meeting. I have had a recent death in my family that I haven't told many people about and I've been tasked with making funeral arrangements, and I keep getting emails all day. I'm doing my best to stay present, but it's really hard right now'? Can you see why it's crucial that you make an observation rather than an assumption? This response can remove any need for progressing the conversation further through the process. What started as a feedback conversation can become a support conversation.

Let's assume for now, though, that their response is in agreement with much of what you have observed. For example: 'Yes, I know I was distracted. I was just trying to get on top of my emails because I feel really overwhelmed, and I checked out during the meeting'.

Coach/redirect

Here is an opportunity to discuss what needs to change or look different. Your response here can go one of two ways. More often than not I believe a leader's default approach should be to coach. In the short term, it may be faster and easier to tell someone what they should do next, but the long-term payoff of helping a person develop their problem-solving capability far outweighs the little time you gain.

Generally, it's time to coach when it's an opportunity for the person to learn, and when they have the skills and information required to solve the problem, or when it's an opportunity for you to learn when you don't have all the information or skills required to solve the problem. It's time to redirect when the person lacks the essential information required to make an informed decision, or when it is an issue of safety for you, the person involved or others.

A simple adjustment between telling and asking can determine how this conversation will progress.

As a coaching moment, you could ask them, 'What could you do differently next time?'

As a redirecting moment, you could tell them, 'What I would like you to do differently next time is...' For example: 'Thanks for acknowledging that this behaviour didn't align with our expectations of each other. In future, if you feel like you will be distracted by your computer, perhaps you could try bringing a paper notebook and pen to avoid this situation happening again'.

Agreement

Once you have talked through the outcome you would like to see from this conversation, it is important to create a shared agreement of what will happen next. In each conversation, there is an agreement from the team member relating to the decisions and behaviours that will follow the conversation. There is also an agreement from you as the leader to follow through on any of the decisions or commitments you made to them during the conversation.

For example: 'I want to clarify our commitments to each other moving forward from here. I'll organise a time to catch up with you and discuss your workload, because I can see it's challenging for you right now. You said you are happy to start using a pen and paper during meetings instead of your laptop to avoid the distraction of your emails. Is this something we can both agree to?'

Appreciation

If you have ever been on the receiving end of a difficult piece of feedback, you'll know that no matter how well it is delivered, there's always a chance you will be left questioning where you stand with the person who delivered it. As a self-professed overthinker, I have gone down the rabbit hole of thinking 'I'm no good' regularly, and it couldn't have been further from the truth. I'm not suggesting you wrap your team in cotton wool, but closing the conversation with a little bit of belief and confidence can go a long way in helping a team member to feel empowered going forward. While some behaviours can be disappointing, it's important to remember that people are not their behaviour and that every person is capable of change. Remind them of that.

For example: 'I want to say thank you for taking on this feedback. I value your contribution to the team, and so when we didn't get to hear it, we noticed it. I have full confidence that you'll take this feedback on and keep doing great work on this team'.

Follow through

You can take a deep breath and congratulate yourself for tackling a difficult conversation head on. In my experience, the conversation in reality rarely lives up to how challenging we make it seem in our mind. However, while the conversation is done, the process is not. What happens after the conversation is just as important.

Here are a few more things you can do after the conversation.

Record

Regardless of how big or small the conversation may seem, it's important to keep a confidential record that it took place. This is not about building a case against a person; rather, it's about ensuring you have a record to identify recurring themes of conversations that take place to better support a person. There are rare but very real circumstances in which you may be required to have a more formalised conversation, and the quality of your records can vastly improve this process for you. You may find yourself having the same conversation multiple times before a more formalised process needs to take place. By having a record of the previous conversations, you avoid the situation in which a person claims they are ignorant of any issues having arisen.

Action

During the conversation, you and your team member made commitments to each other. It's important that you follow through on your commitment to them. If you agreed to set up a meeting with them, arrange it early. If you said you would support them with additional training or learning, then keep them informed on the progress.

Notice

I've always loved the concept of trying to 'catch someone doing something right'. Some behaviours are simple redirects. They are easy to change, and this can be done immediately. Other behaviours require a small set of changes in order to embed the overall change. I think it's important to acknowledge progress and not just the outcome. In our example from earlier, how would you catch that team member actively contributing to the meeting? How could you notice when they choose to leave their laptop at their desk? When did they provide a great suggestion to the team? Acknowledge the little differences.

Celebrate

When you catch someone doing something right, take the moment to meaningfully and intentionally celebrate it. You don't need to buy them a gift or throw them a parade, but use your words intentionally. Link the behaviour back to the conversation and show the person that you notice their effort.

Evaluate

After a period of time, you will want to evaluate whether or not the outcome you are working towards has been achieved. Has this cultural inconsistency been addressed, or is this issue still present? Is this a problem that can be solved, or does it require an alternative strategy? I first heard this idea from Andy Stanley: 'Is this a problem to solve or a tension to manage?' He says that if a problem can be resolved, it usually doesn't show up again. In contrast, if a problem that is solved continues to show up, it's worth considering whether this is in fact a tension that needs to be managed. Take a moment to reflect on whether you are happy with where things are or where they are heading.

Communicate

Whether you are happy with the progress of your team member or whether they are not living up to their agreement, it's imperative to communicate and let them know. We're generally a lot more intentional about letting someone know that they need to keep improving, but we also need to let them know when we are happy with the outcome of their behaviour. Remove the room for interpretation and make it clear.

How great leaders value important conversations

Important conversations come with the territory of being a leader. But have you ever felt like an important conversation you needed to have with your leader wasn't valued by them? How did it make you feel? If the answer is 'Not great', that's motivation to think more about this. You can make sure the person on the receiving end of a confronting conversation feels valued by you.

You can assign high 'value' to important conversations through simple actions. Leaders who do these actions, not only strengthen the trust of their employees but build a culture in which their team is fully empowered to speak up when there's something going on.

Here are five simple ways that great leaders place high value on important conversations.

They are punctual

Being punctual says, 'Your time is important to me'.

As simple as it may sound, arriving on time to a meeting places value on both the person and the conversation. This means that when a meeting is scheduled for 10:30 a.m., you are seated, prepared and ready to go by 10:30 a.m., not just walking through the door or wrapping up your last meeting.

Avoid the temptation to fill your day with back-to-back meetings. Plan for the unexpected by putting time margins around your appointments. Assume that someone will try and 'catch you for five minutes' while you are on your way somewhere. You can be certain that your day will have interruptions, but when you have allowed margins, these interruptions won't throw you off course.

They leave time

Allowing enough time says, 'This meeting is important to me'.

Allow more time than you think you need. This will stop you from 'clock watching' or needing to 'cut this short', which only makes a person feel like you have somewhere more important to be. You should always allow more time than you think you'll need for a difficult conversation. Create space at the end of the meeting to agree on action steps and the plan forward. Invite the team member to ask questions and seek clarity on anything that was discussed. Don't just allow time for what you want to say – make time for everything that needs to be said.

They think location

Considering location says, 'Your privacy is important to me'.

Where you meet can make or break an important conversation. If an employee is experiencing some type of conflict with their fellow team members, it goes without saying that taking them aside in an open-plan office to discuss the conflict will impact on their ability to be open and transparent.

Create opportunity for people to be transparent. This might mean booking a private room in another building or meeting off-site to discuss confidential matters. Thinking this through before you arrive extends the invitation for the person to share freely and openly.

They stay focused

Staying focused says, 'Your content is important to me'.

Be careful not to hijack an important conversation with your own agenda. Topics raised in the meeting may trigger other concerns and tasks that need to be addressed or accomplished. Be sure to stay on point with the purpose of the conversation. Take time to ask more questions and avoid jumping in with quick-fix solutions.

They eliminate distractions

Eliminating distractions says, 'You are important to me'.

Distraction is simply divided attention. To place value on a person and an important conversation, give that person your undivided attention. Set your phone to 'do not disturb', because otherwise we all know the buzzing in your pocket will get the better of you. Manage expectations and create boundaries for those who need to reach you. Let them know you will be uncontactable for an hour and will return their call. Place a 'do not disturb' sign on the door so people don't interrupt.

It's the simple actions that show our teams we care. It's the small courtesies that place value on a person and a conversation.

For some people I talk to, delivering a hard truth to a team member can feel like strapping on a set of boxing gloves. It doesn't have to be that way. Most of the leaders I know care deeply about helping their teams become better; I assume that you do, too. These conversations are about building people up, not beating people up. I've learned that if your goal is to prove you're right, you'll almost always go wrong, but if your goal is to make things right then you'll almost never go wrong.

Here are a few quick tips to wrap this up:

- **Be proactive:** Address things quickly.
- **Be specific:** Give practical examples of your observations.
- **Be clear:** Make the link between the behaviour and the culture.
- **Be humble:** Ask for their input and recognise you could be wrong.
- **Be ready:** Know what you want to look different moving forward and take ownership for your part.

And most importantly, when it comes to hard conversations, just be kind.

Action steps

Remember this

- If you want to change cultural inconsistencies, then you need to confront them.
- The confrontation conversation is about making feedback less difficult – taking the time to address cultural inconsistencies to ensure every person knows what is tolerated and what is not. This accountability flows through the team in every direction.
- Feedback isn't comfortable, but it is always valuable.
- No news is not good news. Your team values helpful feedback.
- The conversations you don't have may end up reinforcing the culture you don't want.
- Leaders show that they value important conversations by being punctual, allowing the right amount of time, thinking through location, staying on topic and removing distractions.

Try this

Prepare yourself to have the confrontation conversation. Familiarise yourself and your team with the 'think through, talk through, follow through' framework:

- Before the confronting conversation, 'think through': consider the purpose of the conversation, the outcome you want to achieve, the support they may need to change, and the temperature and timing of the discussion, so that you can have a plan going in.
- During the conversation, use the plan to 'talk through': make an observation of behaviour, help them understand the impact of that behaviour, seek their perspective and input, redirect or coach towards the aligned behaviour, seek agreement, and show appreciation.
- After the conversation, be sure to 'follow through': keep a confidential record of the conversation and action any agreements made. Try to notice and catch them 'doing something right' so you can celebrate the progress and meaningfully reward it. After a period of time, evaluate whether the outcome has been achieved, and communicate again.

Work towards this

Early on, the process may feel clunky, but over time you can make it your own and it will feel less scripted. You might find it helpful to bookmark the following page.

Difficult Conversations

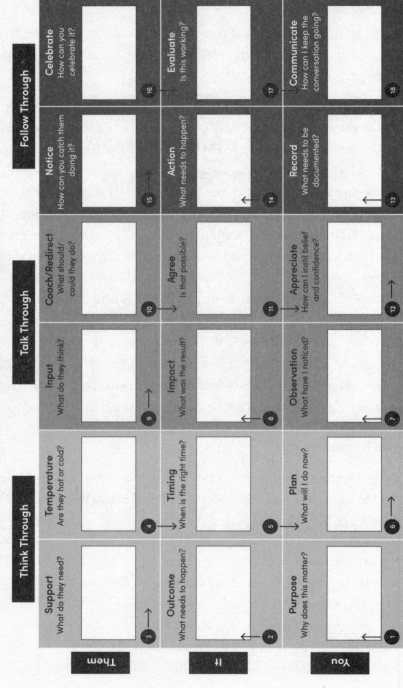

	Think Through		Talk Through		Follow Through	
Them	**Support** What do they need? ③	**Temperature** Are they hot or cold? ④	**Input** What do they think? ⑨	**Coach/Redirect** What should/ could they do? ⑩	**Notice** How can you catch them doing it? ⑮	**Celebrate** How can you celebrate it? ⑯
It	**Outcome** What needs to happen? ②	**Timing** When is the right time? ⑤	**Impact** What was the result? ⑧	**Agree** Is that possible? ⑪	**Action** What needs to happen? ⑭	**Evaluate** Is this working? ⑰
You	**Purpose** Why does this matter? ①	**Plan** What will I do now? ⑥	**Observation** What have I noticed? ⑦	**Appreciate** How can I instill belief and confidence? ⑫	**Record** What needs to be documented? ⑬	**Communicate** How can I keep the conversation going? ⑱

Chapter 10

The celebration conversation

Make recognition more meaningful

'If I do something terrible, tell me. If I do something great,
tell somebody else.' – Lisa O'Neill

Key finding: Nearly half of people leaders said that
a lack of reward and recognition contributes to an
unhealthy culture in an organisation.

Recognition helps people feel seen. Recognition doesn't take long, but it goes a long way.

People repeat and replicate what they see recognised and rewarded. If you want to shape a culture by design then it's not just about pulling people up when they get it wrong, it's also about taking the time to meaningfully and intentionally celebrate when they get it right.

In our quantitative research, we asked people leaders how they shape the culture within their team, and just 38 per cent said they 'reward behaviours that align with how we do things'. When it comes to shaping the culture you want in your team, recognition might just be one of your best under-utilised tools.

O.C. Tanner is an employee recognition company working to improve 'workplace cultures through personalised employee recognition solutions, so people feel appreciated, do their best work, and come to stay'. For the past few years, they have provided powerful insights into the trends, statistics and perceptions that are shaping workplace cultures around the world. Their *2022 Global Culture Report* contains findings from an experiment that highlight both the importance of recognition and the damaging consequences of its absence.

During their exploratory focus group interviews, an employee recounted a personal story in which he stayed late to help a colleague with an upcoming project. This was not something that was required of him, and it was not a project he was directly involved in. Having worked with this colleague for the last year and recognising that she was in need of help, he went over and above to support her. The week after her presentation, she took a moment to recognise a number of people for their help and work on it, but not him. Understandably, he was frustrated, and when asked if he would help her again responded with, 'She can jump in a lake'.

Using this story, the team assigned 6000 employees to a control or treatment scenario in which they were asked about three factors in relationship to the story:

1. the employee's general connection to the colleague
2. their willingness to help again
3. whether they would connect with them outside of work.

For the control group, the helper did not receive recognition for their support. The treatment groups then considered a number of scenarios, which included recognition in the form of a non-monetary ecard, a monetary ecard, public recognition with no monetary reward and public recognition with a monetary incentive. As you can probably predict, the results found that failure to recognise a colleague led to the lowest rating of future support, colleague connection and connection outside of work, while higher levels of visibility and financial incentive led to greater levels of future support and connection.

The group were given a self-evaluation to determine a score out of ten in the three areas of connection to colleague, willingness to help again and connection outside of work. The control group mean scores without any recognition were 4.74, 5.07 and 5.12 respectively. Simply taking the time to publicly recognise the helper's effort *without* any monetary incentive increased these scores to 6.85, 7.19 and 6.79. Intentionally thanking a colleague in the presence of others increased the likelihood that the person would repeat the supportive behaviour by over 40 per cent.

Take a moment to reflect on how you would feel if you were on the receiving end of this scenario. Imagine going above and beyond to support a colleague and receiving no recognition for that effort. You might tell me it wouldn't matter. As a coach and trainer, I regularly discuss the importance of recognition with my clients and sometimes people tell me that it doesn't matter whether they receive praise for a job well done. And yet, that data tells a different story. It's not uncommon to hear accounts of employees who leave because they don't feel appreciated in their role.

According to Gallup's research, recognition or praise isn't as common as we might think. In a US study, only one in three workers strongly agreed that they had received recognition or praise for doing good work in the past seven days. The *2020 Culture Report* released by Achievers Workforce Institute stated that more than a third of employees, when asked how recently they had received recognition, responded that they had only received recognition in the last six months or more.

Are the small number of people who say they don't need recognition simply unaware of what they are missing out on? Have they taught themselves to be self-reliant? What we know from a number of recent studies is that when employees receive regular recognition for their work, they are more likely to be engaged in their role than those who don't. And when people are engaged, not only do they stay longer, but they do better work.

On 25 May 2011, the final episode of *The Oprah Winfrey Show* was aired to audiences. In this episode, Oprah shared a simple insight she gained from more than 30,000 interviews with people from around the globe, which is that every one of those 30,000 people wanted validation:

> 'If I could reach through this television and sit on your sofa or sit on a stool in your kitchen right now, I would tell you that every single person you will ever meet shares that common desire. They want to know: "Do you see me? Do you hear me? Does what I say mean anything to you?"'

At its core, recognition isn't just about helping a person feel valued for their work; recognition helps a person feel seen for their contribution. The old adage, 'If you don't hear from me, you can assume you're doing a good job', simply does not bring out the best in those you lead. My good friend and colleague Rohan Dredge is a leadership and culture expert who taught me this powerful mantra: 'If you see it in them, say it to them'. These aren't just words to him – he lives by them wholeheartedly, and you'll be hard-pressed to find a bigger supporter in your network.

Recognition helps people see

Recognition doesn't just help your team feel seen. It also helps your team see what you're working towards more clearly. All but one of the people leaders in our qualitative interviews believed they could clearly articulate their organisation's values and how they live them out day to day. Only four, however, believed their team members could do the same. What was most interesting was that the leaders who worked in organisations that regularly recognise when employee behaviour aligns with company values and culture were more confident in their team's ability to articulate how they live out the values day to day. When the right behaviours are consistently and intentionally rewarded, everybody gets a clearer picture of the team you are trying to create.

One of the participants shared their experience:

'We do a monthly vote for someone in your team, the person who stood out to you, your MVP, but it is all centred around our values... whoever wins the most wins $100, but that is sort of irrelevant – it's more about having your name read out and public acknowledgement. We've just had our company conference and I was presenting on our people and culture. We thought it would be a trick question to ask, 'Who knows what our values are?' in a poll. Ninety-one per cent of them got it right, and the 9 per cent who didn't were the new starters. We had four people whose first day was at the conference. Then we went through each of the values and went through some examples of the ways of doing it, and everyone was throwing in their examples as well. So, I would say my team would be pretty confident [to articulate the values and how they live them out].'

When you take time to meaningfully reward and recognise the behaviours that build the team you want, you bring your values and culture to life. Another participant in our interviews shared a simple recognition practice they call their 'Amps' program:

'The thing that has done that the best in communicating those values is definitely what we call our "Amps" program, which is the recognition program. So, every recognition is mapped against one of our organisational values. I think if we didn't have that, I'd be a bit stuck for what our values are. When we were talking about our values earlier, I could bring them to mind literally because I had nominated Amps awards just before this meeting. I think it's one of those really subtle ways of communicating to the organisation what we value. Outside of that, we have all the standard ways of communicating values, including our annual reports, any documentation in our training modules. But I've been a part of organisations that have done that in the past and it's not necessarily been a way to recognise behaviours that come as a result of the values. This organisation is where I've seen it done really well. They take it seriously when you exhibit one of these behaviours and they reward you for it.'

It doesn't require a huge budget or even a lot of time to start celebrating people for their contribution to culture.

A conversation with Nikki

Nikki Beaumont is the founder and CEO of recruitment company Beaumont People, which exists to connect people with organisations that empower them to do meaningful work and to create more opportunities for meaningful work in Australia. In 2020, Beaumont People was recognised as the fourth best place to work in Australia for companies with under 100 employees, and was also recognised as Australia's second-best place to work in the Professional Services category of the 2021 AFR BOSS Best Places to Work list. I wanted to learn a little more about what went on behind the scenes of an organisation like that and reached out to Nikki for a brief interview on what makes their culture special. Among many of the things you would expect, it was apparent throughout the conversation that celebration played a critical role in shaping their culture:

'I think what keeps our culture alive is we talk about and celebrate these things [the expected behaviours] on a regular basis. People will verbally talk about it, people will comment and celebrate, and make mention, and share, and so that keeps certain elements of our culture, the way we do things, alive.'

One of the ways in which Beaumont People celebrate is something they call 'magic mentions', a practice that began over 20 years ago when Nikki was General Manager of Recruitment for the 2000 Summer Olympics in Sydney:

'During the busiest time recruiting for the Olympic games, those last few months, the volume of work was so huge, we were so stretched beyond capacity that our Friday end-of-day Magic Mentions just kept us all going. The individual recognition and celebration of each other was enough to keep our spirits high and set us up for another week. It was so well received and so impactful that I have continued to do that with my team 22 years on!

'"Magic mentions" is where every single person within the organisation puts forward a mention of somebody else within the organisation that's done something great or worth being recognised for. And so that in itself, I find, is a great way of continually supporting our culture and the way that we do things, and what is recognised and celebrated. Because someone will go, "I just want to recognise that person for doing this in this way, or supporting me in this way, or overcoming that in this way", or whatever it might be, and new people hear, that's how we do things around here. But it also inspires everybody within the organisation, because they're hearing these things regularly. It's being talked about all the time.'

When it comes to recognition, though, Nikki told me it's important that what you celebrate is intentional. It's not just about celebrating one thing or what work gets done, but focusing on how the work gets done and what impact that has created – that has been an important aspect of their celebration:

'We make sure we celebrate a variety of things which are important to our success and our culture, and not focus on one thing. It's easy to celebrate sales or profitability, but we ensure we also celebrate and share other aspects that matter too, such as feedback from clients and candidates. The fact that one team might be the most profitable is not necessarily what is celebrated, but rather what they did for this client, or the feedback we've received from candidates, or how they've supported other teams or individuals.'

When you take time to recognise how a person is doing their work, not only the work itself, it opens up a new avenue of recognition that can help a person feel appreciated in their role. Nikki shared a recent example of an employee who had not been getting their financial results for the work they had been putting in:

'We often have conversations with people who may not be hitting their financial targets for a period of time, which causes them great concern or distress, even, so we make sure we look deeper into all the aspects of their role that lead to their success and acknowledge that. We have a saying, "Let's control what we can control," and we understand that sometimes it takes a while to see the results for your efforts.'

I think there is something to be said for the importance of rewarding progress, not just completion, or rewarding alignment even when the outcome was not what you were expecting. What Nikki and the team are rewarding is behaviours that build that culture and outcomes they want.

While celebration was the core focus of my discussion with Nikki, it's important to note that celebration does not negate the need for important conversations about cultural inconsistencies:

> 'I really believe that your culture is impacted by everybody…
> I mean, there's a saying, isn't there, that "the behaviour you walk past is the behaviour you accept". And we talk about that quite regularly, because it is our job to go, "Now hang on, we don't do it like this, that's not the way that we do things around here".'

One simple but clever recognition tool they use is their 'Beaumont Bests'. Nikki described it as being like a book of *Guinness World Records* for their business:

> 'One thing we love to celebrate is our "Beaumont Bests". These are things like the highest financial performance indicators on an individual, team and company basis. Every month, in our all-company branch meeting, we celebrate which milestones have been beaten. These Beaumont Bests become people's goals and aspirations: they are often talked about and create a real culture of drive and success.'

There are a couple of things that I love about Nikki's approach to building culture. The first is the way in which she empowers her people leaders to take on the role of building culture within their teams through their own culture charters:

'We have a Beaumont People culture charter, but each team is encouraged to create their own version of a culture charter that is specific to how they want to operate as a team. It doesn't replace the central one but rather identifies behaviours and actions about how they work together and support each other. For example, it might include things like, when a client calls, if your colleague is not available, somebody must take the call and do what they can to help the client, and at least understand what their needs are rather than have a message left that might be urgent and not picked up for some hours.

'I love that and firmly believe that different teams can have their own different cultures within a larger organisational culture.'

As a leader within your organisation, you can shape the culture of your team, but it's important to ensure that that culture aligns with the culture your organisation is aspiring to have.

The second thing I love about Nikki's approach is her commitment to making the conversation about culture ongoing:

'Every week, we have an hour or so training and development for everyone within the business, which goes through all aspects of our work – including our core values, how we work – and helps keep everyone on the same page and constantly evolving as a business. We call it CPD: Continuing Professional Development.'

Not only is culture talked about regularly, it's also embedded into every part of their employee experience right from the beginning:

'Part of their induction is they have to have an element of training from at least half of the people in the business. So, the training isn't done by the training manager. It's all done collectively between us. We get them to go and interview other people within the business and go, "Tell me about the culture; what do I need to know about the culture around here?"

'We also ask different people in the business to be part of the interview process when we are hiring and make it a key part of the discussions. We also like potential new people to meet some some of their new team members and specifically ask them about the culture within the team and the business.'

If you asked a new person to go and interview each member of your team about what it's like to work in your team, would you feel confident in their response? That's the kind of cultural clarity we are aspiring to in this process.

On the question of whether or not culture can be influenced, Nikki said:

'I absolutely believe that yes, culture can be influenced, you can change your culture, and we have done that and will continue to do that as needed. Ours has evolved beautifully over time, but there are times when I can look back and think, "That wasn't a great culture then". Maybe I wasn't as purposeful as I could have been to change it, maybe I should have read this book... maybe I didn't have the right leaders leading the culture. I think you need to have "listening ears" in your organisation to hear what your culture is really like. It's important to build relationships with people so that they can be completely open and honest with you, not just about culture but about everything!'

Don't underestimate the power of celebrating the behaviours that help build the culture you want, and don't overthink how much time, budget or resources you need to make it a reality. Whether it's a public award at an event or just a personal 'thank you' to a colleague, a little recognition can make a big difference.

Having the conversation

You don't need to search too deeply in any organisation or team to catch someone doing something wrong, or to point out a problem that needs to be fixed. But when was the last time you intentionally went looking to catch someone in the act of doing something right? This idea, to 'catch people doing something right', has always stayed with me since reading the classic book *The One Minute Manager* by Ken Blanchard and Spencer Johnson.

But what do you do when you catch them? How do show your appreciation in a meaningful way? And more than that, how do you use that opportunity to proactively build and shape the desired culture of your team or organisation?

When thinking through recognition, you will find it helpful to break it down into three important parts:

1. **Who** should be the one to deliver the recognition?
2. **What** is the behaviour being rewarded?
3. **How** will you recognise and reward this behaviour?

Who

There were a number of valuable insights in the *2021 Engagement and Retention Report* produced by Achievers Workforce Institute, which studied over 2000 American and Canadian workers and the role of recognition. They found that more than two thirds (69 per cent) of employees believe that their relationship with their manager would improve if their manager took the time to recognise them more.

This is consistent with O.C. Tanner's findings about the link between recognition and connection: when it comes to recognition for those on your team who model the behaviours that build the culture you want, each person on the team should feel empowered to have this conversation.

In a conversation I had with a leader recently, they shared a simple but helpful initiative they have for recognition, which they call 'works of ART'. 'ART' is an acronym for 'appreciation, recognition and thanks'. They encourage team members to 'get creative' in their recognition of one another and provide cards that colleagues can give to one another when they spot great behaviours in action. While it's important for recognition to flow top-down, it's just as important that it goes around your team and each person has the opportunity to call out the best in each other.

One of the participants in our qualitative study shared how they empower each member of their team to recognise the great things in their team:

> 'The first five to ten minutes of our stand-up meeting is what we call a "kudos session". There are eight values, four of which are our organisation's values, four of which are (our team's) values, and we shout people out for the things that have happened in the past week aligned to those values.'

It's important that each person on the team has an avenue for recognising the other members of their team, or you as the leader for modelling the behaviours you agreed to. But as the leader, you have an additional responsibility, because your words have weight. In a 2016 Gallup workplace study, employees were asked to recall who gave them their most meaningful and memorable recognition. They found that the most memorable recognition comes most often from an employee's manager (28 per cent), followed by a high-level leader or

CEO (24 per cent), the manager's manager (12 per cent), a customer (10 per cent) and then peers (9 per cent). Not surprisingly, people want to hear from the leader that they interact with the most that they are doing a good job.

When I speak to leaders who are facing morale issues or consistent performance issues in their team, one of the first questions I'll ask is, 'When was the last time you celebrated the good in your team?' Many times the answer is, 'Not recently'. Even in challenging times, there's good to find, and it means the most coming from you.

What

Taking the time to celebrate a behaviour on your team lets the people around you know what you value. So, it's important to remember that when you celebrate, you communicate. When it comes to recognition, it's worth taking the time to consider whether the behaviour you are rewarding is something you would like to see more of.

Let me give you an example of what I mean. Celinda was an in-house video editor who was delegated a last-minute project for an important event. The process of filming, editing and then creating the finished product was no small feat, but rather than informing her manager that there was too much involved in the project to deliver it in such a short amount of time, she decided to take on the work. Celinda spent countless hours editing in the week leading up to the event, working late into the night. Her colleagues noticed she was the first to arrive in the morning and the last to leave at night. They knew how much effort she was putting into this. On the final night before it was due, she made the decision to sleep on the floor of her office while the video was exporting, just to make sure it was ready for the next day. Celinda's manager knew that she had gone above and beyond to deliver on the work, and so she took a moment during the event to publicly acknowledge her and appreciate her for the hours she had put in. For the rest of the afternoon, different leaders from the business came up and commented on how valuable the video was and how much they appreciated her effort and work. She left the event feeling deeply valued for her effort and work. Her colleagues also noticed the extra attention she received for that kind of effort.

It seems like an innocent story, and of course there are times when people need to pull together to accomplish a lot with a little. But there are two major issues with this kind of behaviour. The first is what happens when she is faced with the same situation again later. She immediately thinks back to the positive feelings of being rewarded for her work and how great it was to receive so much affirmation from colleagues, and she defaults to saying 'yes' instead of speaking honestly about the situation. The second issue is that the public recognition signals to her colleagues that people who say 'yes' to their own detriment are the example to follow, or that the business values people working late into the night to deliver on their work.

Everything you reward tells a story about what you value. It's important to make sure that it's a story you want told.

How

There are four ways you can ensure that the recognition conversation is helping shape the culture you want:

1. **Make it specific:** It's important to be as articulate in your praise as you would be in your criticism. Don't generalise recognition. Start the conversation by making an observation about the behaviour that you would like to recognise. Consider the following:

    - What did you see or hear?
    - What are the specific positive behaviours that you want to affirm?
    - What caught your attention?

Finish this sentence: 'Hi [insert name], I just want you to know I noticed that...' Let's use a scenario in which team member Zhu has noticed that new starter Ray has been struggling to familiarise himself with a new Customer Relationship Management (CRM) system and has taken the initiative to go and support him to learn. To make the praise specific, you might say: 'Hi Zhu, I just want you to know I noticed that you have been helping Ray learn our CRM system. He told me how much easier it has been to navigate having spent time with you going through all of the advanced functions'.

2. **Make it meaningful:** Make sure the person you are recognising is clear on the impact of their behaviour. How did this positive behaviour impact you or your team? Most importantly, why was this action meaningful to you or to your team? How can you let this person know that their actions made a real difference? Consider the following:

   - What did their actions enable you or your team to do more or less of?
   - How did it make you or the team feel?
   - Who was helped as a result of these actions?

   Finish this sentence: 'That was valuable to me/our team because...' Continuing the conversation with Zhu, you might make the praise meaningful by saying: 'That was valuable to the sales team because they were working on an important pitch, so having someone else to support on the admin side of things meant they were able to focus on the deal. It also meant that, as a team leader, I was able to focus my time on the customer and answering any important questions. I know you have a lot of your own personal work to deliver on, and you taking this on was over and above what was expected of you'.

3. **Make it intentional:** Affirming positive behaviour intentionally shapes and reinforces the team culture you are trying to build and links back to the shared behaviours and expectations of your team. How does this specific behaviour align with the agreements you have made as a team about the culture you are working towards? Consider the following:

    · What are your team's shared expectations that this aligns with?
    · What are the behaviours and actions linked to that expectation?
    · How does this behaviour align with those expectations and behaviours?

    Finish this sentence: 'This matters because the type of team we all agreed we are trying to build is...' For example, making Zhu's recognition intentional might sound like this: 'This really matters because the type of team we all agreed we are trying to build is one in which we have each other's back, and what you did was a great example of this in action'.

4. **Make it personal:** Say 'thank you' in a way that is personal. We give and receive appreciation in different ways. For one person, a public 'thank you' in a team meeting is valuable; for another, it may be embarrassing. Some people appreciate a gift; others find meaning in words. Understand how a person feels valued and express your thanks in their own language of appreciation. Consider the following:

    · How does this person feel valued?
    · What would make this 'thank you' feel more personal?
    · Could I ask them how they would like to be recognised and build something together?

Finish this sentence: 'I want to say "thank you" by…'

Finishing the recognition and making it personal in our example with Zhu might look like this: 'Zhu, I want you to know how much I appreciate what you did. I know you said you enjoy going to the movies but haven't been lately, so I want to say "thank you" by arranging a couple of movie tickets for you'.

Too much of a good thing?

As a child, I remember being given a gold coin for pocket money in return for cleaning my room. In the beginning it was a reward for behaviour. Over time it became an expectation: I wouldn't clean my room unless I received the reward. My parents had to teach me the importance of ownership and responsibility. I learned to clean without the reward. As an adult, I don't need a reward or even recognition to clean my house. I understand the responsibility. But even still, when someone takes the time to notice what I've done and meaningfully says 'thank you', I can't deny the positive impact it has.

I'm not for a moment suggesting that every good behaviour needs a gift, or that a person on your team deserves a parade for doing their job. I am saying that if recognition isn't commonplace in your team, then there's an opportunity to do something now that communicates loudly what you value. Who doesn't appreciate it when someone says, 'I see you and thank you'?

Management expert D.D. Warrick said, 'Leaders can make all kinds of statements about the type of culture they desire, but ultimately employees will respond to the behaviours that they see valued, recognised, and rewarded'. You can say, 'We want a culture of safety', but are you rewarding safe practices? You can say, 'We want a culture of openness', but are you affirming people who speak up? You can say,

'We want work-life balance,' but are you rewarding those who leave work on time at the end of the day?

When you celebrate, you communicate.

Action steps

Remember this

- Recognition doesn't just help people feel valued, it also helps them feel seen.
- People repeat and replicate what they see recognised and rewarded.
- The celebration conversation is about making recognition more meaningful – taking the time to meaningfully reward the behaviours that build the team culture you aspire to, ensuring that the right behaviours are repeated.
- When giving recognition, think through *who* should deliver the feedback, *what* behaviour is being rewarded that you want repeated, and *how* you will recognise and reward the behaviour.
- You don't need to reward every good behaviour, but the right behaviours should be intentionally rewarded.

Try this

- Look for opportunities to catch the people on your team living out the clarified behaviours you agreed would help to create the culture you want, and meaningfully recognise and reward them.
- Think through the forums in which great work can be celebrated. Could it be a standing agenda item to recognise and reward the people on your team, or could you implement an ongoing nomination system that empowers people to recognise their peers?

- When you recognise the behaviour, make it:
  - specific: what happened?
  - meaningful: what was the positive impact?
  - intentional: how does it link back to your culture?
  - personal: how would this person feel most recognised?

Work towards this

After the celebration conversation, the person on the receiving end of the feedback should feel valued and appreciated; however, they should also have a clear understanding of how this behaviour shapes the culture your team agreed it is working towards.

Chapter 11

The dark side of culture

Don't accidentally build a cult

'Toxic culture is like carbon monoxide: you don't see or smell it, but you wake up dead!' – Dr Samuel Chand

---

Key finding: Just 16% of people leaders currently receive ongoing training in how to shape culture within their teams.

On 26 March 1997, deputies of the San Diego County Sheriff's Department arrived at a house in Rancho Santa Fe in San Diego to find 39 members of the UFO religious group Heaven's Gate who had tragically taken their own lives. Founded in the early 1970s, Heaven's Gate was a cult group that held to the central belief that they could transform themselves into immortal extraterrestrial beings by rejecting their human nature, which would enable them to ascend to heaven, referred to as the 'Next Level' or 'The Evolutionary Level Above Human'. Their leader, Marshall Applewhite, told his followers that he was the second coming of Jesus Christ, that God was an alien, and that they were living in the end times. They were led to believe that, by freeing their souls from their body, they could ascend to a spacecraft flying in the wake of the Hale–Bopp comet – which at that point was passing by Earth – to be taken to their new home in space.

As absurd as this cult philosophy seems, it was compelling enough to cause a group of people to follow it to such an extreme that they were willing to sacrifice their own lives.

I hope that by this point in the book you are on board with the importance of culture, that you have a clear strategy for designing the culture you want and that you know some of the ingredients that will help you shape it and live it out day to day. But with the good there is also the bad, and for every light there is a shadow. Culture is no exception. Culture at its best is empowering, inclusive, unifying and attractive. The conversations in this book are about shaping a way of doing things that embodies this. At its extreme, though, and used the wrong way, culture can cross a dangerous line and create a way of doing things that becomes controlling, isolating, divisive and destructive.

Taking the 'cult' out of culture

So, at what point does the desire to create a strong, healthy culture cross the line into unhealthy cult-like behaviours? And how do we make sure we never cross that line?

Dr Janja Lalich, a former Fulbright scholar, is a professor emerita of sociology at California State University, Chico. In the 1970s she spent more than ten years as part of a radical Marxist political group that was going to change the world through a workers' revolution. The Democratic Workers Party in California, she later came to realise, was a cult. Today she is best known as a foremost expert on cults and coercion, charismatic authority, power relations, ideology and social control. As an international authority in the field, she has appeared in several court cases as an expert witness on coercive control or undue influence. Via a very early morning Zoom call in December 2021, I was fortunate to have a conversation with her to learn a little more about some of the ideologies and features that cults share, and how we can ensure we build a strong team culture without crossing the line into destructive cult-like behaviours.

Dr Lalich recounted her personal connection to the Heaven's Gate suicides, which occurred while she was in grad school:

'I knew a lot about that cult and had met a number of people who'd been in a long time. And I was actually working with a family whose daughter had gotten recruited. In fact, I had to call, I was the one who called them to tell them, like, "Be careful if you turn on the TV; you're going to see your daughter saying goodbye". So, I was in grad school at the time just about to start the dissertation work, and my advisor and my committee chair said, "Okay, this is it, this is what you're going to do, this is perfect. This is your dissertation".

'And then he said, "But even better would be to do a comparative study rather than just one case study. So, why don't you compare Heaven's Gate to the cult you were in, because you couldn't have two more different cults, right? You've got this UFO cult hoping to leave the world, and then you've got this political cult that wants to change the world". And so that I think gave me another opportunity to really step back from my own experience and examine the cult, the group, whatever – the party – from a researcher's point of view, a sociologist's point of view. And through that comparison is how I came up with my bounded choice theory and framework.'

Dr Lalich's bounded choice theory identifies four specific features that cultic groups share, which I first read about in her book

Escaping Utopia: Growing Up in a Cult, Getting Out, and Starting Over. These are the four features:

1. **A transcendent belief system:** While it may not always be a higher power, cult groups nearly always gather around an ideology that creates a 'right way'. This belief system becomes the focus of the group's members, who strive to transform themselves to become more dedicated believers. This insiders' way leads to an enforcement of behaviours that ensure total devotion, and eradication of behaviours that challenge this belief system or its leaders. This results in a fierce distrust or even a hatred of outsiders.

2. **Systems of control:** In cult groups, there are certain systems of control that are more overt and obvious. These systems are designed to create what Dr Lalich describes as a 'bounded reality', in which a set of strict rules and enforced behavioural norms enclose members in a tightly controlled universe. These could include norms around dress, communication, diet, sexual habits and even who you may or may not spend time with. These systems of control in essence seek to strip away any sense of individuality from members.

3. **Systems of influence:** Systems of influence are much less overt. When enough people are dedicated to the systems of control, then there is a stronger peer influence that begins to emerge within the group. The dedication of some followers may cause them to shun or shame others who step out of line, leading those members to lose a sense of belonging or inclusion. In systems of influence, the group leader relies on much more human emotions such as shame, guilt, love and the desire to do better to emotionally manipulate or gain leverage over the cult's members.

4. **A charismatic authority:** A cult group's leader will find ways to keep members engaged in the group through displays of charisma, vision and emotional manipulation. Dr Lalich likens it to 'hero worship' or 'the madly-in-love feelings that erase our good sense'. In many cults, the leader attracts an inner-circle leadership who gain this charisma by proxy, making the leader even more inaccessible and admired and yet making the group stronger by having a group of leaders as enforcers.

Dr Lalich recounted to me her experience of this charisma by proxy:

'I was in the inner circle, and I was one of the top leaders in my group. So, everything I did was to uphold the standards of the party, or lead courses that were indoctrinating people and teaching them to behave in these certain ways and become this perfect little cadre fighter. So, the middle-level leaders or the middle-level managers are there to constantly be reinforcing, hopefully acting as good examples of the goals of the group – again, which are supporting the leader in one way or another.

'So, being at that level of leadership, in my world, we call that "charisma by proxy". Because they're so-called blessed by the leader, they become sub-leaders; they, in a sense, carry the charisma of the leader, and people are expected to follow them just as they would if it was the leader telling them. Because in many groups, people never see the leader. They certainly never meet the leader, especially in the large groups. So, you've got to have these other people who can stand in his or her stead and keep everybody in line.'

Side note: even in cults, you can't underestimate the role of the middle leader and their contribution to the strength of the organisation!

How to avoid accidentally building a cult

Before you're tempted to dismiss everything you've learned up to this point because you're afraid of becoming an accidental cult leader, let me put your mind at ease. Let's talk about how to stay far away from the culty side of culture.

Culture is iterative, not sacred

We can change it if it doesn't serve us.

In a cult, there is no attempt to change or adapt its transcendent belief system as the group evolves and changes. The belief system or doctrine is held up as sacred. Dr Lalich explains:

> 'The transcendent belief system is the only way, right? So, it goes back to that idea of, "We're the only ones, we're perfect, we're special". And it has the answers to everything. That belief system answers everything for you. In the cult context, it's the past, the present and the future. It reshapes your world view.'

When you're building culture, it serves the direction and purpose of the organisation and your team, not the other way around. You don't find your purpose in the culture or use the culture to make sense of the world. Over time, your culture will become a process of iteration and evolution, which means it doesn't need to look the same today as it did a year ago or even a month ago. Culture iteration is not heretical as it would be in a cult. You can and should work to shift the culture if it is no longer in the best interests of the team or the business. 'That's just the way we've always done things', or 'That's just how we do things', is not a valid justification for sustaining a culture that is no longer in the best interests of the people.

There is nothing wrong with upholding a set of values or expectations that you are proud of and your team is committed to, as long as you can recognise that these are just *a* way of doing things and not necessarily *the* way. Dr Lalich explains:

'Certainly you want to engender pride in your workers, and pride in their work, and pride in what your company's doing, but if you do it to the extent that everything else is shit, that's not good, because then that leads into that us-versus-them mentality.

'I remember back in the '80s all the businesses had what were called "quality circles", which was something that started in Japan. And at that time, everybody was about how successful things were in Japan. So, we used to, once a week – I don't think it was once a day – we'd have these quality circles where we'd have to all sit around and basically talk about how to improve the business. But it was to the point where it had nothing to do with how to improve conditions for the workers… It was only how to make us perform better so that the boss can earn more money, so the profits will increase, but that didn't affect us as the staff in any way, shape or form that was beneficial to us.

'So, it was this very divided… in a sense, the us-versus-them was inside the workplace. There [are] the bosses, and then there [are] the worker bees. And we don't talk about what's good for the worker bees. We only talk about what's good for the bosses and the profit margin. And so, it was like, "Oh yeah, quality circles. What are we talking about here?"'

A culture by design is not only in the best interests of you, the leader, or of the organisation – culture is a shared experience that is good for everybody. The goal isn't to create a new belief system for people, but rather to surface the belief system that already exists and determine whether it is helpful or useful – and if not, how it may need to change.

Practically speaking, here are some things you can do:

- Go back to your expectations and behaviours regularly and check in with your team to see whether they still hold true and are in service to the team.
- Regularly examine some of the long-held traditions, rituals or norms in the team or business and consider whether they are still relevant and useful.
- Examine your language and consider whether it needs to evolve to become more inclusive.
- Create a safe space to challenge ways of thinking and upheld beliefs.
- Regularly remind the people on your team that there is room for different perspectives, beliefs and ideas.

Culture is resilient, not fragile

We can handle robust scrutiny of our culture.

In a cult, unquestioned devotion is rewarded, and scrutiny is labelled as blasphemy. When you're building culture, welcome questions and robust discussion, knowing that the culture you are building can stand up to it. Reward critical thinking and value informed commitment from your people. Healthy discussion and dialogue are critical to building a resilient culture, according to Dr Lalich:

'I think having an openness to open discussion, open questioning [is critical]. When I was a professor, I used to always say there's no question that's stupid. There are no stupid questions. Ask your questions. Challenge me. Put forth your argument. And I think if you're open to that, unless you have somebody in your group... that's totally trying to undermine

you in some kind of way and take over the business or something like that, but short of that, one should be open to that
kind of discussion.'

In cult groups, Dr Lalich says, there is no questioning the way things
are done and no challenging:

'A huge part of the training or the indoctrination is to get the
person to internalise this idea that you don't challenge, you
don't criticise, you accept things as they are. If you don't like
it, tough. And there [are] different ways in which people may
be punished if they break that rule. But there are many, many
both overt and unspoken rules about things like that. And
certainly, no criticism, especially of the leader or of the current
program of action, or whatever it is – it's sacrosanct. You don't
touch it, so that's certainly very characteristic of a cult.'

When it comes to challenging the way things get done, it's important
not just to seek input from people on your team but to go further
and invite people into the conversation from outside your context and
give them permission to challenge it:

'So, in a business context, that would do the same thing of
basically enclosing people into what I call the "self-sealing
system": "We're so great that we've got to keep it all together,
and we're keeping it all together by not letting anything
in and not looking to the outside". So, shutting down any
kind of input would definitely be detrimental to a business
organisation. Things are changing all the time in the outside
world, even if you aren't. So, if you're not able to keep up with
that, you're going to be stuck in time. So, I think it's important
to have that openness, and to have transparency, and to have

checks and balances, so that you can grow and stay relevant as a business.'

Who could you invite to give an external perspective and share honest feedback about your culture? What forums allow people to share openly and honestly about the current state of the culture?

Practically speaking, here are some things you can do:

· Invite people to ask questions and challenge the culture.
· Share your culture document with people from outside your team and invite feedback.
· Invite external team members to interview your team about the culture of your team.
· Provide formal and informal channels that allow honest feedback.
· Carefully consider how you respond as a leader when the culture is challenged.
· Celebrate critical thinking in your team.

Culture is oneness, not sameness

We can have alignment without agreement.

Building a culture means placing value on diversity (in all its forms), not trying to eradicate it. Culture is about finding unity in diversity. We can think, feel and act differently while aligning around and sharing a common purpose, direction and vision. It's possible for me to value your perspective even when I don't share your preference. Cults focus on replicating sameness, but culture is about fostering oneness. You don't need to agree with everything in a team, but you can align around a core set of shared expectations. Culture is about being aligned at the core while remaining inclusive at the edges. We value people feeling safe to bring their whole selves to work without the fear of judgement or shame.

In *Escaping Utopia*, Dr Lalich paints a picture of an unhealthy removal of individuality:

'In the narcissistic and malignant environment of cults, obeying the leader is essential if you want to stay in good graces, or be allowed to stay at all. Individuality or dissimilarity from the leader, then, is unsafe and unwise. Accordingly, it's common for cult members to emulate the leader – talk like him, act like him or use the same gestures.'

In my conversation with Sameer B. Srivastava from the Haas School of Business at the University of California, he told me about a test that is common in the US when it comes to recruiting for culture fit, known as the 'Wichita test':

'If I got stuck at the airport in Wichita with this colleague, would I have enjoyed talking to him or her at the bar while I'm waiting for my delayed flight to take off? And what the Wichita test and other kinds of so-called cultural fit tests are often about is some measure of social similarity. Does this person look like me, have a similar background, and so on. So, it's often a way that organisations just reinforce inequality. It's because people are just hiring people who look like them.'

The sense of unity and oneness in a team does not come from eradicating differences – it comes from creating a compelling shared purpose and experience.

Practically speaking, here are some things you can do:

- Celebrate the differences in your team.
- Help the people on your team feel comfortable to share their perspectives.
- Regularly invite external perspectives into the conversation.

- Seek to uncover your own unconscious biases.
- Ask more questions.
- Learn more about what makes the people on your team unique.
- Invite greater diversity of thought into your personal network.

Culture is shared, not forced

We want choice, not control.

In a cult, members are told what to value, and the rules and expectations come from above. Those rules and expectations seek to control. When members do not act appropriately, they are shamed or made to feel guilty for not living up to this transcendent belief system. Great cultures, on the other hand, create a shared ownership of what the team values and expects of one another. They invite people into the conversation and do not exclude them from it. When people miss the mark, they are supported and reminded of the shared aspiration and their potential, and not publicly shamed or put through extreme punishment.

It's important to remember that the five conversations discussed in this book are all shared conversations. The expectation conversation aims to produce a set of shared expectations or values that align the team. The clarification conversation is not about creating behavioural rules, but rather deciding collectively on what behaviours, if focused on, will help move the needle closer to the culture the team aspires to – they are for guiding, not oppressing. The confrontation and celebration conversations are designed to point people to a set of shared commitments made to one another, which should flow in every direction – from leader to team, team member to leader and team member to colleague.

In my discussion with Sameer about the communication conversation, he raised an important point about the fine line between language that is used for empowering culture and that which is used for social control. He highlighted this through an example about diversity, equity and inclusion:

> 'In general, I understand what you're saying, and I agree with you that deliberatively changing language can be a powerful tool… But you can also imagine being a frontline worker and hearing this and rolling your eyes. And I think in today's world, with a lot of the language changes happening around diversity, equity, inclusion and belonging, particularly here in the US, there are employees who roll their eyes.
>
> 'You're trying to create a culture of inclusiveness, but the way you're doing it is by standardising the way we talk and actually making it less inclusive to people who might talk in a different way or think about these issues in a certainly different way. Then it can quickly slip into feeling like social control, language as a means of social control.'

The goal of cultural language is to empower people with the words to talk about your culture, not to control the way they talk about it. If the language you are using to describe the culture does not empower you or your team, then give people the freedom to change it.

Practically speaking, here are some things you can do:

- Include your team in the culture conversations.
- Empower every person on your team to call out cultural misalignment up, down and across.
- Promote a shared accountability of the culture, not an enforcement of the culture.
- Ensure that nobody in the group is above the rules, including the leader.

- Create cultural language in collaboration, and regularly review whether it serves the purpose of empowerment.

Culture has often been described as the 'way *we* do things around here'. It is collaborative and embraced. Cults are often marked by leaders telling people the 'way *you* will do things around here'. It is dictated and enforced.

Both are about creating a 'way', but I think we all know which one we would prefer.

Action steps

Remember this

- You are building culture, not forming a cult.
- Culture is the way *we* do things around here, not an enforcement of the way *you* will do things around here.
- Culture is collaborative and embraced, not dictated and enforced.
- Culture is iterative, not sacred, which means we can change it if it doesn't serve us.
- Culture is resilient, not fragile, so it can stand up to scrutiny from people internally and externally.
- Culture is oneness, not sameness, so we can have alignment without agreement.
- Culture is shared, not forced; so we want choice, not control.

Try this

Discuss with your team and agree on a cadence of review for your culture statements. This could be monthly, quarterly or every six months. When you meet, consider the following questions:

- Does this still ring true for us?

- Is this still the culture we aspire to create?
- Are these behaviours still relevant or our top priority?
- What progress have we made, and what is getting in the way of progress?
- Do we think anything needs to be added to this?
- Are we missing a valuable perspective that needs to be included?
- Are we still committed to creating this culture?

As a leader, intentionally seek out internal and external perspectives and voices that can evaluate and provide helpful feedback about your team culture.

Work towards this

The goal of this conversation is to gain ongoing commitment to the culture you are working towards. Culture conversations are ongoing conversations, not moments in time.

Chapter 12

The path forward

Become a Culture Champion

'You don't have to be great to start, but you have to start to be great.' – Zig Ziglar

---

Key finding: Just 3% of people leaders feel completely confident about building great culture.

There was a popular TV ad campaign for milk back in 2010 in Australia by Pauls. A man walks into his local corner store and asks for a bottle of milk. The shopkeeper responds with: 'Low fat, no fat, full cream, high calcium, high protein, soy, light, skim, omega 3, high calcium with vitamin D and folate, or extra dollop?'

To which he replies, 'I just want milk that tastes like real milk'.

As you consider the path forward for shaping the culture of your team, the good news is that you have options. You can start anywhere you like. The bad news is also that you have options, and you can start anywhere you like. In his 2004 book *The Paradox of Choice: Why More Is Less*, Barry Schwartz argues that too many choices can actually be detrimental to our psychological and emotional wellbeing. As you and your team think about the areas of culture that will create the best return, there's potential for the decision to feel a little overwhelming.

In our interviews with people leaders, there were a couple of common questions that came up:

1. Where do I focus my attention on culture?
2. How much time should I invest in culture?

Where you start is less important than the decision to start – but let's look at where you might consider starting, nonetheless.

Culture builders and culture killers

When we asked people which ingredients contribute towards a healthy team culture, these five were the most popular. If you're looking for a good entry point, these might just be a great place to start.

1. Collaboration and teamwork (53 per cent)

Not surprisingly, over half of the people leaders we surveyed told us that collaboration and teamwork were an essential part of healthy culture. As you explore your shared expectations and behaviours, consider asking questions that bring out the ways you prefer to work together as a team.

Here are some questions you could ask:

· Where and when are you at your best?
· How do you prefer to collaborate?
· How do you prefer to share information?
· What brings out the best in you in a meeting?
· What brings out the worst in you in a meeting?
· What does being a good team member look like?

One of the top five culture killers was 'negativity from leaders or team members' (49 per cent). It could be worth taking the time to consider the role that optimism and positivity play in your team dynamic. Take time to clarify what negativity means to people on the team and what expectations they have about dealing with stress or setbacks.

2. Leaders who are visible and approachable (52 per cent)

You can't follow an invisible leader. You might prefer to be a leader who is behind the scenes, but your team wants to see you. They want to know that you are available and approachable when they need you. One of the top five culture killers in our research was 'an absent or disconnected leader' (48 per cent). In your culture conversations, explore with your team what it means to be present. What are their expectations of you around being visible and approachable?

Here are some questions you could ask:

· How often do you like to hear from me? In what way?
· What does it mean to be approachable?
· What do you need to hear from me?
· How often should we meet?

3. Open communication and feedback (52 per cent)

Each person on your team will have preferences around the way they like to communicate and the frequency in which they like to receive feedback. Having a conversation about the culture of communication in your team can help you set realistic expectations early. In our research, a 'lack of accountability' (45 per cent) in the team was seen as one of the top five culture killers. What are the ways in which the team can foster a sense of shared accountability? When team members don't feel empowered to speak up, a team will eventually break down.

Here are some questions you could ask:

- How often do you like to be communicated with?
- In what way do you like to be communicated with?
- What are your expectations around feedback?
- Who do you regularly need communication from or with?
- How do we deliver hard truths in this team?

4. Trusting relationships (50 per cent)

A lack of trust is the number-one culture killer, according to our research. Half of people leaders told us that they identify a healthy culture by the trusting relationships that exist. How trust is built looks different for each person. Take time to explore some of the areas that help establish trust in your team.

Here are some questions you could ask:

- What can I do that instils confidence in you?
- What helps build trusting relationships in this team?
- How is trust broken and restored?
- How do you feel trusted?
- What should you do when you can't share all the information?

5. Clear and realistic workload expectations (49 per cent)

People want to know they are doing a good job, which means having clear and realistic workload expectations and clear measures of success. Forty-six per cent of the people leaders in our research told us that unclear or unrealistic workload expectations were a key ingredient for an unhealthy culture.

Here are some questions you could ask:

- How do we measure success in this team?

- Where do you go if you are unclear on work expectations?
- How do you prioritise work?
- What do you do when you're struggling?
- What are your expectations of each other around sharing workload?

Investing in culture

Dollar cost averaging is an investment strategy that seeks to eliminate some of the impact of volatility in the market. By breaking down a large investment into small increments, over time you run a much smaller risk of loss than if you were to invest a lump sum before a fall in the market. The idea is that you do a little bit consistently rather than big chunks sporadically.

While it's tempting to get caught up measuring the time investment into culture, it's not always a helpful measure. Our research told us that most people leaders spend an average of three to four hours a month investing in culture. Our culture champions typically spent eight hours or more. And yet, almost nine in ten leaders told us they felt like they should be doing more.

Rather than asking, 'How much time should I invest in culture?' instead consider asking, 'How can I ensure that culture is consistently central to our most important conversations?'

The World Health Organization recommends an hour of movement every day for adults in order to maintain a healthy lifestyle. They use the phrase 'every move counts'. That movement might be a run, a walk, a swim or simply choosing to take the stairs instead of the escalator. If you hold the mindset that every move counts, you go looking for ways to make a move. Keep the conversation about culture front and centre in your team and you will be surprised at how easy it can be to invest in it. Go looking for ways to make a move and invest in your culture.

Someone to be

I'll always remember the conversations I shared with Lincoln at that little Italian restaurant in the town where I grew up. As my first mentor, he taught me a lot about life and leadership that I'm extremely grateful for today. One of the phrases etched into my mind was, 'You teach what you know but you reproduce what you are'. I've heard it attributed to a few different people, but I believe he was quoting leadership expert John C. Maxwell. It's a phrase that has stuck with me because it has always framed the way I approach the conversation about leadership and culture. You don't just *do* culture, you need to *be* the culture. You can invest all the time and effort into the conversations that provide a road map for the team you want, but undermine its progress through your daily actions or decisions as a leader. I would say that values get a bad rap in an organisation for this reason. More often than not, they are simply lifeless words on wall.

In our research, we asked people leaders whether they believed their leaders demonstrated the organisation's values and, alarmingly, just 30 per cent strongly agreed.

When we interviewed people leaders about what they believed their key responsibility was in culture-building, there was a consistent theme of modelling the culture. Here are some of the responses:

· 'My responsibility is, "Do I embed the traits or values I want
   to see in a healthy culture?" That's been something I've
   worked really hard at, to remain aligned with the values of the
   organisation and get on board with what they're going after. Does
   what I say align to those values, and am I actually instilling the
   values in my team as well? I think I have a huge responsibility
   in that. And challenging the other leaders in my organisation
   as well. Are we making the right decisions? Something that my
   organisation does really well is encouraging those constructive

conversations at any level, and so I've had my GM challenge me on challenging him, and he actually encourages that behaviour.'

- 'Shaping culture is providing an example. The culture I would like my team to demonstrate is something I have to live by. I provide an example as a benchmark for my team.'

- 'I think it's really important to model the behaviour you want to see. I talked about [our value] "Love your neighbour as yourself", and the "yourself" part is self-care… We have lots of deadlines, everyone is busy, there is always lots of work, so I want to make sure I am modelling a healthy culture of not expecting overtime all the time… If they saw me online all time, they would have an expectation that they should be online all the time… [It's about] being quite intentional about not just discussing and having conversations but actually modelling it for my team.'

- 'Communicate expectations clearly and role-model that behaviour. For example, I don't email past 5 p.m. because I've learned over the years that things can wait. I role-model the behaviours I'd like to see.'

What we know about culture is that there is an element of social learning, whereby we take notice of what the people around us do. We look to leaders and role models to not just tell us the way but show us the way.

The 11 per cent

If I ask you to think of a leader who has made a significant impact on you personally or professionally, who is the first person that comes to mind? In my practice, I describe these people as the 'remarkable leaders'. 'Remarkable' originally comes from a French word that means 'to take note of'. Remarkable leaders are those who you take note of in your mind because they leave an impression on you. It's hard to pinpoint, but there is something different about those people. They stand out in your memory for a reason. They are outliers among the people you encounter. The reason I do what I do is that I hope, in some small way, I can help develop more of those kinds of leaders so they become less of an anomaly.

Gallup's research found that about 'one in ten people possess high talent to manage'. While they do admit that many people have *some* of the necessary traits, there are significantly fewer people that have the unique combination of talents they say are needed to help 'a team achieve the kind of excellence that significantly improves a company's performance'. They say that this 10 per cent, when put in manager roles, 'naturally engage team members and customers, retain top performers, and sustain a culture of high productivity'. In less discouraging news, they also found that 'another two in 10 people exhibit some characteristics of basic managerial talent and can function at a high level if their company invests in coaching and developmental plans for them'.

When we looked for trends that appeared in our research, exploring the beliefs and experience of people leaders when it came to culture, we found a similar group of outliers, only it was a group of 11 per cent. They didn't respond the same way as the average people leader to the questions we asked. This 11 per cent strongly agreed that:

- the values of their organisation were clearly communicated to everyone
- the values are demonstrated by the organisation's leadership
- they were able to describe the values and how they live them out every day
- the values were more than words – they have clear behavioural expectations.

We called this group our 'Culture Champions'. They are a small group of outliers who are currently working in organisations where the expectations of them are clearly communicated, the behaviours are explicitly defined and everybody lives them out every day. When these elements of culture are present, people leaders are twice as likely to rate the culture of their organisation as 'excellent'. When we compared their responses with those of the average people leader (who we labelled the 'Moderate Manager'), we identified a clear trend.

Here are 11 things our 11 per cent can teach us about culture.

1. Culture can be influenced

Almost two in five Culture Champions (38 per cent) 'strongly' or 'somewhat' disagreed with the statement 'Culture is not something that can be influenced, it just happens', compared to 19 per cent of Moderate Managers. As a leader, it's important to regularly examine your beliefs under a microscope and determine whether you still hold them to be true, or more importantly, whether or not those beliefs are actually helpful to hold. Those who don't believe culture can be influenced are unlikely to influence it.

2. Culture is in the little things

Culture Champions understand that culture is built through the seemingly insignificant daily decisions. Collectively, more than nine in ten people leaders (95 per cent) agreed that culture is the outcome of lots of little decisions made over time, and we found that Culture Champions were more likely to strongly agree with the statement.

We rarely celebrate finishing one page in a book. We don't get excited about losing just one kilogram. We don't get the productivity crown for responding to one email. And yet, small decisions can have big consequences. Think about a missed decimal point in a spreadsheet, or using plain flour instead of self-raising flour in a recipe. If you reflect on a decision that had big consequences, you'll likely find that it was the product of a series of small (and, at times, seemingly inconsequential) decisions. Culture Champions understand the importance of the seemingly insignificant decisions in building a culture by design, so they pay attention to the details.

3. Culture is not static

Culture Champions were more likely than Moderate Managers to strongly agree that culture is dynamic and changes (35 per cent, compared to 26 per cent). The culture you have today may not be the culture you have tomorrow. Consider how the events of 9/11 changed the culture of airline travel, or how the COVID-19 pandemic transformed the culture of remote working. Culture Champions know that when the culture no longer serves the team, they can change it.

4. Culture needs a leader

Culture Champions place as much responsibility on themselves as they do on the head of the organisation. Collectively, people leaders see communicating culture as their primary role. They also believe they hold the main responsibility in living it out day to day and addressing the cultural inconsistencies in their team. While 75 per cent of people leaders believed that the head of the organisation is responsible for setting the culture, our Culture Champions believed that they carry equal responsibility (74 per cent). This even supersedes the responsibility of the C-Suite or executive team. Culture Champions are also more likely (54 per cent) than Moderate Managers (44 per cent) to see creating a healthy culture within their team as the most important part of their role.

You might be working in an organisation that hasn't yet taken the time to articulate its culture clearly, but that doesn't have to stop you from working with your team to shape the culture you want right now. While some people sit around and complain about the culture they have, Culture Champions are working to build the culture they want.

5. Culture is the key to success

Culture Champions are more likely to believe that there is a strong link between culture and the overall success of an organisation. While almost all people leaders (99 per cent) 'definitely' or 'somewhat' believed that culture plays an integral role in the overall success of an organisation, almost nine in ten Culture Champions (88 per cent) 'definitely' believed this, compared to seven in ten (72 per cent) Moderate Managers. More specifically, Culture Champions were a lot stronger in their recognition of the impact culture had on an organisation's ability to achieve its goals. Culture Champions know that if they are going to produce results and achieve goals, culture needs to be central to the conversation.

6. Culture needs trust, transparency and learning

Culture Champions were more likely than Moderate Managers to see trusting relationships (76 per cent, compared to 47 per cent), learning opportunities (64 per cent, compared to 39 per cent) and transparent leadership (67 per cent, compared to 42 per cent) as essential ingredients of a healthy organisational culture. Culture Champions care about their relationships. They want their team to feel confident in them, and they want their team to feel that they are investing in them.

7. Culture needs clarity

Culture Champions know that in order to shape culture, you need clear behavioural expectations that show you what to reward and confront. When we asked people leaders to identify the areas that contribute to an unhealthy culture in an organisation, Culture Champions were more likely than Moderate Managers to see lack of clarity around organisational values (63 per cent, compared to 39 per cent) and expected behaviours (62 per cent, compared to 38 per cent) as negatively impacting organisational culture.

The way Culture Champions created clarity to shape culture was through rewarding the behaviours that aligned with how they do things (64 per cent, compared to 34 per cent of Moderate Managers) and clearly communicating cultural expectations (65 per cent, compared to 37 per cent of Moderate Managers), while half shaped culture through confronting behaviours that did not align (54 per cent, compared to 36 per cent of Moderate Managers).

Interestingly, Culture Champions were more likely than Moderate Managers to see a lack of reward and recognition (67 per cent, compared to 40 per cent) as a key contributor to an unhealthy culture.

8. Culture can be challenged

Culture Champions feel empowered to speak up when they see something that needs to be addressed. For more than nine in ten people leaders (93 per cent), honest and timely feedback conversations are commonplace in their organisation. But there is room for improvement, with less than two in five (37 per cent) strongly agreeing with this statement.

Culture Champions were twice as likely to strongly agree with the following statements:

- 'Honest, timely feedback conversations are commonplace here.'
- 'I feel empowered to speak up when I see a culture and values misalignment.'
- 'I feel comfortable delivering difficult feedback to more junior team members.'

- 'I feel safe to challenge the culture in my organisation.'
- 'I feel comfortable delivering difficult feedback to more senior team members.'

Culture Champions feel confident to speak up when they see something that needs to change. They know that, in doing so, they are helping shape the culture they want.

9. Culture takes time

Culture Champions are twice as likely as Moderate Managers to invest eight hours or more per month into shaping the culture in their team (46 per cent, compared to 21 per cent). People leaders most commonly invest three to four hours per month into shaping the culture in their team. Interestingly, despite Culture Champions' higher investment into culture, they are equally as likely as Moderate Managers to believe they should do more. More than two in five Culture Champions (43 per cent) 'definitely' believe they should do more, compared to 47 per cent of Moderate Managers. Culture Champions know that you can't change a culture overnight.

10. Culture training pays off

Culture Champions know that an investment in culture training makes a difference. The people leaders in our study who received ongoing training were more likely to have a clear understanding of their role in shaping culture, have the skills and knowledge to do it and feel empowered to carry it out.

11. Culture shifts performance

Culture Champions know that when the culture is strong, people are empowered to do their best work and perform at their best. When we asked leaders to rate the performance of their team and their organisation, Culture Champions were twice as likely as Moderate Managers to rate their team and organisation as 'excellent'.

Remember – the culture you're working *to* also has a *from*

When I work with leaders as a coach to help them communicate messaging, particularly around change, I always remind them that where they are bringing people on the journey *from* is just as crucial as the place they are taking them *to*. You have to understand where people are right now and what has led them there in order to help them make the shift to where you need them to be. The same is true of culture. You need to understand the culture you *have* as much as you need to be intentional about creating the culture you *want*.

In my earlier conversation with Dan Mottau, he described culture as having organisational memory:

'Culture is also organisational memory, which is to say that organisational memory lives within the fabric and it's very subversive in many ways – that certain events that have occurred, even prior to half the workforce's experience, [will] still pervade, if not challenged and eased out. It has history. It has stories. It has mythology.

'And you don't necessarily want to get rid of it at all. In fact, it can be a huge advantage. Where it becomes problematic is in dysfunction, where that organisational memory is what you want to remove from the business. And the behaviours you want to instil are those you are focusing on [in] the present and observable, but they constantly clash with the organisational memory.'

As you reflect with your team on the culture you aspire to create, take time to examine whether your existing culture in the team or your organisation could be working against you.

If the team culture you have right now is not the team culture you want, you can change it – but don't presume it will be easy. For a period of time, there will be what Steve Pressfield describes in *The War of Art* as 'the life we live, and the unlived life within us'. Between these two lives, he says, stands resistance, a wrestle between the way things are done now and the way you strive for things to be. Don't stop. Don't go back. Each decision, each conversation, each interaction is an opportunity to reinforce the team you aspire to have and the leader you aspire to be.

Action steps

Remember this

- Culture needs somewhere to start and someone to lead.
- Where you start and what you focus on is important. What is most important, however, is the decision to start.
- If you're struggling to find an area of focus, begin with the culture builders:
  - collaboration and teamwork
  - leadership visibility
  - communication and feedback
  - trust and relationships
  - workload expectations.
- Culture is 'be', not just 'do'.
- Culture Champions believe that culture can be influenced and needs a leader – that it is a series of small decisions that create change over time. They know that culture plays a crucial role

in success and shifting performance, but it needs clarity, trust, transparency and learning. They understand that culture takes time, improves with investment and can be robust enough to be challenged.

- Every culture you're working *to* also has a *from*.

Try this

- Culture is not just about doing. Ask your team to consider what it would look like to *be* the culture you are aspiring to, and to share their responses in your next meeting.
- Share the top five culture builders with your team and facilitate a conversation about how these contribute to the culture you are shaping. Try asking the following questions:
  - How do we collaborate at our best as a team?
  - How often should we meet?
  - How often do you like to hear from me, and in what way?
  - What contributes to trusting relationships on this team?
  - How do we measure success on this team?
- Take a moment to personally reflect on the 11 characteristics of a Culture Champion. How many qualities do you align with? What further training, support or learning would you need to better understand your role in leading culture?
- Set a meeting with a sample of people from your team and organisation to better understand and explore the existing culture. Try asking the following questions:
  - What words would you use to describe our culture right now?
  - What do we celebrate in this organisation?
  - What has experience taught you that we 'don't do'?
  - What behaviours do you see that are commonplace in our organisation?

Work towards this

Culture is not just something you carry alone as the leader – you are working towards shared ownership, in which your team feels a sense of responsibility for achieving the cultural outcomes. By the end of this conversation, you may realise that there are missing elements that need to be discussed, which is also a helpful outcome.

A final summary

Reinforce what you've learned

The 'fade-out' is a musical technique that dominated the pop music industry for nearly four decades from the late 1950s – in most part due to technology and convenience. We're quick to forget it was commonplace until you find yourself on a wedding dance floor and the music begins to fade out as you're busting your best moves to a classic.

My biggest fear in writing a book is that the concepts within it remain clever ideas on a page that never see the light of day, like a 1990s banger that excites for a moment and finishes on a subtle and slow fade-out. Don't make culture a moment in your team – make culture a movement. Let the culture conversations grow, evolve, adapt and strengthen over time with your people.

If you're looking to keep these conversations fresh in your memory, here is a summary of the ground we have covered in this book.

Culture is the key to making differences work at work

We are all a little bit different. This is both valuable and chaotic. We bring these differences with us into the workplace, and our teams are more valuable because of them, but they need to work at work. Culture is the key to making these differences work at work. For many teams, culture remains unspoken and undefined, and as a result, their culture remains unclear and undefined. When we take time to communicate clearly and surface the unspoken, we can create alignment around a common way of doing things that helps our teams thrive.

Culture makes an impact

When culture is strong, we attract and retain the best people. We adapt more quickly, collaborate better and decide faster, which helps us accelerate progress and achieve our goals. We create teams in which people feel safe to show up fully, knowing they will be protected from harm. We help people find a greater sense of belonging, share their perspectives with a greater degree of confidence and deliver results that shift the bottom line in business.

Culture isn't easy

While culture can feel overwhelming in the number of ways you could define it, some common themes exist to help us make sense of it. Rather than being overwhelmed by what you don't know, focus on what you do. Instead of getting hung up on how to define it, make sure you know how to apply it.

Recognise that your team is consistently learning from what they observe around them and using that information to make sense of and interpret what the unspoken expectations are that enable them to belong and function in your team. These norms determine what is accepted, rejected, encouraged and discouraged within the group. Over time, these norms can become so deeply ingrained that we become completely unaware of their existence. Becoming aware of them enables us to take responsibility for how intentionally culture is shaped.

You may not be able to influence whether culture exists, but you can influence what kind of culture exists. Everyone is responsible for culture, but culture needs a leader. You are that leader. Culture can be influenced, but it needs intentionality. At times, culture may leave you with more questions than answers and more content than confidence, but with the right strategy and a commitment to the process, you can create the culture you want.

Culture needs a conversation

There's a conversation about culture that precedes the culture conversations. As a leader, you play a valuable role ensuring that foundation is strong. Ensure your team conversations are built on trust, vulnerability, empathy, curiosity and safety before you tackle these five:

1. **The expectation conversation** is about making the unspoken spoken – taking the time to surface the unspoken expectations you have of each other and the organisation has of you to discover what you value and hold in high regard. As you discover these expectations, you can 'chunk up' to define their common themes.

2. **The clarification conversation** is about making the invisible observable – taking the time to clarify the behaviours that demonstrate the shared expectations. 'Chunk down' your expectations to the point where everyone can leave the meeting and know what to do. Agree on the behaviours that will help move the needle in the direction of the culture you and your team aspire to create.

3. **The communication conversation** is about making the words a language – taking the time to create internal team memes that are both memorable and meaningful so that each person on the team feels empowered to talk about the culture in a consistent way. Through personal stories and rituals, these words come to life.
4. **The confrontation conversation** is about making feedback less difficult – taking the time to address cultural inconsistencies to ensure every person knows what is tolerated and what is not. This accountability flows in every direction of the team.
5. **The celebration conversation** is about making recognition more meaningful – taking the time to meaningfully reward the behaviours that build the team culture you aspire to, ensuring that the right behaviours are repeated.

Culture needs focus and visibility

Once you have captured the outcomes of your conversations, pick three and make them easy to see. When everything is a priority, then nothing is a priority. Which three expectations and behaviours are most important to you and the team, and how can you make them visible to everyone in your day-to-day work?

Culture has a dark side

For all the good that culture can create, you need to be aware of when culture goes too far. Culture is shared, not enforced, which means it can be changed if it does not serve the team. Culture can handle being challenged by the team. It celebrates difference; it does not seek to eradicate individuality.

Culture needs somewhere to start and someone to lead

If you're feeling overwhelmed about where to start, or you want to focus on the areas that are most important to shape a healthy culture, start with the culture builders. Focus on collaboration and teamwork, leadership visibility, communication and feedback, building trust and making workload expectations clear and realistic. Culture isn't just *do*, it's *be*. It needs role models, Culture Champions who think differently.

Culture has a 'from' and a 'to'

Organisational memory means there will be resistance from the culture you have to the culture you want. Don't give up. Put culture at the centre of everything you do as a team and watch what it can do for you.

The right conversations can shape the culture you need and help to create the team that you want. Conversations don't happen in a book, though: this is just a guide. You can create a world-class team culture by design. What really matters most is that you start.

Say it again

'When you are tired of saying it, people are starting to hear it.'
– Jeff Weiner

The conversations in this book are a beginning, not an end. The conversation about culture is never done.

When you know they haven't got it,
When you don't think they've got it,
When you aren't sure if they've got it,
When you think they might have got it,
When you know they've got it,
When you think you've said it enough,
When you're sick of saying it,
Say it again.

Because people are just starting to get it.

About the author

Shane is a Queenslander by birth, Melbournian by choice, curious by nature and creative at heart. He has spent the last decade developing remarkable leaders, teams and cultures.

He is an expert in leader communication, blending his experience in business and psychology to help leaders communicate, connect and collaborate more effectively in order to bring out the best in those they lead. Shane is passionate about helping leaders have the conversations they need to create the teams they want.

As a speaker, coach and trainer, Shane has partnered with some of Australia's most well known and loved businesses across the public, private and not-for-profit sectors.

His coaching helps individuals and teams better understand what makes them exceptional and how they can leverage that to achieve individual and collective outcomes.

Shane is a Gallup-Certified Strengths Coach and author of *Lead the Room: Communicate a Message That Counts in Moments That Matter.*

Acknowledgements

To my dad, who always told me to be a leader, not a follower. To my mum, who showed me that you can be both. To my brother, who is always there when I get it wrong, and my wife, who inspires me every day to get it right. To the countless people whose investment in me has shaped these words, thank you.

References

Preface

David Foster Wallace, *This Is Water: Some Thoughts, Delivered on a Significant Occasion, about Living a Compassionate Life*, Little, Brown, New York, 2009.

Shane Michael Hatton, *Lead the Room: Communicate a Message That Counts in Moments That Matter*, Major Street Publishing, 2019.

Chapter 1: We're all a little different

Karl Kristian Flores, *The Goodbye Song*, 2021.

David Rock, Heidi Grant and Jacqui Grey, 'Diverse teams feel less comfortable – and that's why they perform better', *Harvard Business Review*, 22 September 2016, <hbr.org/2016/09/diverse-teams-feel-less-comfortable-and-thats-why-they-perform-better>.

Frans Johansson, *The Medici Effect: What Elephants and Epidemics Can Teach Us About Innovation*, Harvard Business School Press, Boston, 2006.

Phone Calls with Clever People, 'Frans Johansson on the power of diversity to drive innovation', podcast, 3 December 2021, <shanemhatton.podbean.com/e/frans-johansson-on-the-power-of-diversity-to-drive-innovation/>.

Victor E. Sower, Jo Ann Duffy and Gerald Kohers, *Benchmarking for Hospitals: Achieving Best-in-Class Performance Without Having to Reinvent the Wheel*, ASQ Quality Press, 2008.

Dominic Powell, 'The big bong: how Jim Kouts turned Off Ya Tree into a $30 million business', *SmartCompany*, 11 February 2019, <smartcompany.com.au/entrepreneurs/influencers-profiles/jim-kouts-off-ya-tree-business/>.

Chapter 2: The unseen advantage

Abby Ghobadian and Nicholas O'Regan, 'The link between culture, strategy and performance in manufacturing SMEs', *Journal of General Management*, vol. 28, no. 1, 2002, pp. 37–56.

Nate Dvorak and Ryan Pendell, 'Culture wins by attracting the top 20% of candidates', Gallup, 28 June 2018, <gallup.com/workplace/237368/culture-wins-attracting-top-candidates.aspx>.

Gallup, *State of the Global Workplace: 2021 Report*, 2021.

Hays, *Salary Guide FY21/22: Australia & New Zealand*.

Amy Edmondson, 'Psychological safety and learning behavior in work teams', *Administrative Science Quarterly*, vol. 44, no. 2, 1999, pp. 350–383.

Elizabeth Medina, 'Job satisfaction and employee turnover intention: what does organizational culture have to do with it?', Master's thesis, Columbia University, 2012, <static1.1.sqspcdn.com/static/f/1528810/23319899/1376576545493/Medina+Elizabeth.pdf>.

PwC, *Global Culture Survey 2021: The Link Between Culture and Competitive Advantage*, 2021, <pwc.com/gx/en/issues/upskilling/global-culture-survey-2021/global-culture-survey-2021-report.html>.

HBR IdeaCast, 'Creating psychological safety in the workplace', podcast, Episode 666, 22 January 2019, <hbr.org/podcast/2019/01/creating-psychological-safety-in-the-workplace>.

Phone Calls with Clever People, 'Fiona Robertson on a new definition of organisational culture and how to change it to enhance results', podcast, 29 July 2020, <iheart.com/podcast/269-phone-calls-with-clever-pe-69196144/episode/fiona-robertson-on-a-new-definition-69214718/>.

Chris Anderson, *TED Talks: The Official TED Guide to Public Speaking*, Headline Publishing Group, London, 2016.

Carolyn Dewar, 'Culture: 4 keys to why it matters', McKinsey & Company, 27 March 2018, <mckinsey.com/business-functions/people-and-organizational-performance/our-insights/the-organization-blog/culture-4-keys-to-why-it-matters>.

Washington Post Live, 'The Great Resignation with Molly M. Anderson, Anthony C. Klotz, PhD & Elaine Welteroth', 24 September 2021, <washingtonpost.com/washington-post-live/2021/09/24/great-resignation-with-molly-anderson-anthony-c-klotz-phd/>.

Chapter 3: The problem with culture

Michael D. Watkins, 'What is organizational culture? And why should we care?', *Harvard Business Review*, 15 May 2013, <hbr.org/2013/05/what-is-organizational-culture>.

Kellie Wong, 'Organizational culture: definition, importance, and development', Achievers, 7 May 2020, <achievers.com/blog/organizational-culture-definition/>.

Deloitte, *Core Beliefs and Culture: Chairman's Survey Findings*, 2012, <deloitte.com/content/dam/Deloitte/global/Documents/About-Deloitte/gx-core-beliefs-and-culture.pdf>.

Jeff Schwartz, Udo Bohdal-Spiegelhoff, Michael Gretczko and Nathan Sloan, 'The gig economy: distraction or disruption?', *Global Human Capital Trends 2016: The New Organization: Different by Design*, Deloitte University Press, 2016, <deloitte.com/content/dam/Deloitte/global/Documents/HumanCapital/gx-dup-global-human-capital-trends-2016.pdf>.

Willem Verbeke, Marco Volgering and Marco Hessels, 'Exploring the conceptual expansion within the field of organizational behaviour: organizational climate and organizational culture', *Journal of Management Studies*, vol. 35, no. 3, May 1998, pp. 303–329.

Edgar H. Schein, *Organizational Culture and Leadership*, 4th edition, Jossey-Bass, San Francisco, 2010.

John P. Kotter and James L. Heskett, *Corporate Culture and Performance*, Free Press, New York, 1992.

John C. Maxwell, *The 21 Irrefutable Laws of Leadership: Follow Them and People Will Follow You*, HarperCollins Leadership, New York, 2007.

Society for Human Resource Management, *The Culture Effect: Why a Positive Workplace Culture Is the New Currency*, 2021, <shrm.org/hr-today/trends-and-forecasting/research-and-surveys/documents/2021%20culture%20refresh%20report.pdf>.

Jim Clifton and Jim Harter, *It's the Manager: Moving from Boss to Coach*, Gallup Press, 2019.

Chapter 4: The conversations before the conversations

James Nathan Miller, 'The art of intelligent listening', *Reader's Digest*, 127, September 1965.

Ashley Mateo, 'Toughen your running bod against injury', Nike, 9 November 2021, <nike.com/au/a/how-to-prevent-common-running-injuries>.

Edelman, *Edelman Trust Barometer: 2021*, <edelman.com/trust/2021-trust-barometer>.

Adam Hickman and Tonya Fredstrom, 'How to build trust with remote employees', Gallup, 7 February 2018, <gallup.com/workplace/236222/build-trust-remote-employees.aspx>.

Jim Harter, 'Why some leaders have their employees' trust, and some don't', Gallup, 13 June 2019, <gallup.com/workplace/258197/why-leaders-employees-trust-don.aspx>.

The Workforce Institute at UKG, *Trust in the Modern Workplace: Why Is Trust Still Hard to Find at Work?*, 2021, <kronos.com.au/resource/download/45056>.

WorkLife with Adam Grant, 'How to be vulnerable at work without spilling everything, from Brené Brown', podcast, 1 March 2021, <ideas.ted.com/how-to-be-vulnerable-at-work-without-spilling-everything-from-brene-brown/>.

Patrick Lencioni, *The Advantage: Why Organizational Health Trumps Everything Else in Business*, Jossey-Bass, San Francisco, 2012.

Businessolver, *2021 State of Workplace Empathy*, <resources.businessolver.com/c/2021-empathy-exec-summ?x=OE03jO>.

TIME, 'Apple CEO Tim Cook Delivers The 2017 MIT Commencement Speech | TIME', video recording, streamed live 10 June 2017, <youtube.com/watch?v=3NXjUpo-1q8>.

Jim Clifton and Jim Harter, op. cit.

Michael Bungay Stanier, *The Coaching Habit: Say Less, Ask More and Change the Way You Lead Forever*, Box of Crayons Press, Toronto, 2016.

Melissa Harrell and Lauren Barbato, 'Great managers still matter: the evolution of Google's Project Oxygen', re:Work with Google, 27 February 2018, <rework.withgoogle.com/blog/the-evolution-of-project-oxygen/>.

re:Work with Google, 'Determine what makes a great manager', accessed 18 February 2022, <rework.withgoogle.com/guides/managers-identify-what-makes-a-great-manager/steps/determine-what-makes-a-great-manager/>.

re:Work with Google, 'Guide: understand team effectiveness', accessed 18 February 2022, <rework.withgoogle.com/print/guides/5721312655835136/>.

James R. Detert and Ethan Burris, 'Can your employees really speak freely?', *Harvard Business Review*, January–February 2016, pp. 80–87, <hbr.org/2016/01/can-your-employees-really-speak-freely>.

Chapter 5: The expectation conversation

UK Department of Health, 'Liberating the NHS: no decision about me, without me: government response', December 2012, <assets.publishing.service.gov.uk/government/uploads/system/uploads/attachment_data/

file/216980/Liberating-the-NHS-No-decision-about-me-without-me-Government-response.pdf>.

Gallup, 'The 34 CliftonStrengths themes explain your talent DNA', accessed 18 February 2022, <gallup.com/cliftonstrengths/en/253715/34-cliftonstrengths-themes.aspx>.

Paul Davies, *God and the New Physics*, Simon and Schuster, New York, 1983.

Holly Ransom, *The Leading Edge: Dream Big, Spark Change and Become the Leader the World Needs You to Be*, Penguin Group Australia, Melbourne, 2021.

John Henry Wigmore, *A Treatise on the Anglo-American System of Evidence in Trials at Common Law: Including the Statutes and Judicial Decisions of all Jurisdictions of the United States and Canada*, Little, Brown, Boston, 1923.

Chapter 6: The clarification conversation

George Dickson, 'Shopify's Brittany Forsyth on scaling company culture', Bonusly, 13 April 2015, <blog.bonus.ly/shopifys-brittany-forsyth-on-scaling-culture/>.

CISCO, *Engagement Pulse: Discussion Guide*, <cisco.com/c/dam/r/team-development/teamspace/assets/Engagement-Pulse-Discussion-Guide.pdf>.

Chapter 7: The communication conversation

Edgar H. Schein, op. cit.

Bill Chappell, 'Winner of French Scrabble title does not speak French', NPR, 21 July 2015, <npr.org/sections/thetwo-way/2015/07/21/424980378/winner-of-french-scrabble-title-does-not-speak-french>.

https://en.wikipedia.org/wiki/Nigel_Richards_(Scrabble_player)

Sameer B. Srivastava, Amir Goldberg, V. Govind Manian and Christopher Potts, 'Enculturation trajectories: language, cultural adaptation, and individual outcomes in organizations', *Management Science*, vol. 64, no. 3, March 2018, pp. 983–1476, <faculty.haas.berkeley.edu/srivastava/papers/Enculturation%20Trajectories.pdf>.

Richard Dawkins, *The Selfish Gene*, Oxford University Press, Oxford, 1976.

Spotify, 'Being here', accessed 18 February 2022, <lifeatspotify.com/being-here>.

Google, 'Ten things we know to be true', accessed 18 February 2022, <about.google/philosophy/>.

Gabrielle Dolan, *Real Communication: How to Be You and Lead True*, John Wiley & Sons Australia, Milton, Queensland, 2019.

HBR IdeaCast, 'Why business jargon isn't all bad', podcast, Episode 668, 5 February 2019, <hbr.org/podcast/2019/02/why-business-jargon-isnt-all-bad>.

Chapter 8: Pick three and make it easy to see

Chris McChesney, Sean Covey and Jim Huling, *The 4 Disciplines of Execution: Achieving Your Wildly Important Goals*, Free Press, New York, 2012.

Justin Bariso, 'Sheryl Sandberg just gave some brilliant career advice. Here it is in 2 words', *Inc.*, accessed 8 March 2022, <inc.com/justin-bariso/sheryl-sandberg-just-gave-some-brilliant-career-ad.html>.

Alicia McKay, *From Strategy to Action: A Guide to Getting Shit Done in the Public Sector*, Structured Conversations, New Zealand, 2019.

James Clear, *Atomic Habits: Tiny Changes, Remarkable Results: An Easy and Proven Way to Build Good Habits and Break Bad Ones*, Avery, New York, 2018.

Aurecon, 'Australia's first visual employment contracts launched', 5 May 2018, <aurecongroup.com/about/latest-news/2018/may/visual-employment-contract>.

Aurecon, 'Aurecon Attributes', accessed 18 February 2022, <aurecongroup.com/careers/culture/aurecon-attributes>.

Part Three: Keeping the Conversation Going

Maggie Hiufu Wong, 'Taiwan's first "pretend to go abroad" tour takes off with fake flight', CNN, updated 3 July 2020, <edition.cnn.com/travel/article/taipei-songshan-airport-fake-travel-tour-intl-hnk/index.html>.

Chapter 9: The confrontation conversation

Steve Gruenert and Todd Whitaker, *School Culture Rewired: How to Define, Assess, and Transform It*, ASCD, Alexandria, Virginia, 2015.

Crucial Dimensions, 'The cost of avoiding conflict', 16 April 2020, <crucialdimensions.com.au/the-cost-of-avoiding-conflict/>.

Briam J. Brim and Jim Asplund, 'Driving engagement by focusing on strengths', Gallup, 12 November 2009, <news.gallup.com/businessjournal/124214/driving-engagement-focusing-strengths.aspx>.

Denise McLain and Iseult Morgan, 'How fast feedback fuels performance', Gallup, 1 January 2022, <gallup.com/workplace/357764/fast-feedback-fuels-performance.aspx>.

Liane Davey, 'A game plan for that conversation you've been putting off', *Harvard Business Review*, 12 April 2017, <hbr.org/2017/04/a-game-plan-for-that-conversation-youve-been-putting-off>.

Mark Gerzon, 'To resolve a conflict, first decide: is it hot or cold?', *Harvard Business Review*, 26 June 2014, <hbr.org/2014/06/to-resolve-a-conflict-first-decide-is-it-hot-or-cold>.

Chapter 10: The celebration conversation

Christina Chau and Reid Thorpe, *Rethink: 2022 Global Culture Report*, O.C. Tanner Institute, <octanner.com/au/global-culture-report.html>.

Annamarie Mann and Nate Dvorak, 'Employee recognition: low cost, high impact', Gallup, 28 June 2016, <gallup.com/workplace/236441/employee-recognition-low-cost-high-impact.aspx>.

Caitlin Nobes, 'A shocking number of employees feel unrecognized for their work during COVID-19', Achievers, 15 September 2020, <achievers.com/blog/employees-unrecognized-covid/>.

Kevin Fallon, 'Oprah's last show: a recap in quotes', *The Atlantic*, 26 May 2011, <theatlantic.com/entertainment/archive/2011/05/oprahs-last-show-a-recap-in-quotes/239483/>.

Great Place to Work, 'Australia's best workplaces 2020: small (under 100 employees)', accessed 18 February 2022, <greatplacetowork.com.au/best-places-to-work-australia-2020-small/>.

AFR BOSS Best Places to Work, '2021 Best Places to Work winners', accessed 18 February 2022, <afrbestplacestowork.com/2021-winners/>.

Kenneth H. Blanchard and Spencer Johnson, *The One Minute Manager*, Morrow, New York, 1982.

D.D. Warrick, 'What leaders need to know about organizational culture', *Business Horizons*, vol. 60, no. 3, 2017, pp. 395–404, <farapaper.com/wp-content/uploads/2018/10/Fardapaper-What-leaders-need-to-know-about-organizational-culture.pdf>.

Chapter 11: The dark side of culture

Samuel R. Chand, *Cracking Your Church's Culture: Seven Keys to Unleashing Vision and Inspiration*, Jossey-Bass, San Francisco, 2010.

Janja Lalich, *Escaping Utopia: Growing Up in a Cult, Getting Out, and Starting Over*, Routledge, New York & London, 2018.

Chapter 12: The path forward

'Pauls Milk 2010 Ad', video recording, uploaded 1 May 2010, <youtube.com/watch?v=4OtsNWXeCfE>.

Barry Schwartz, *The Paradox of Choice: Why More is Less*, Ecco, New York, 2004.

World Health Organization (WHO), *WHO Guidelines on Physical Activity and Sedentary Behaviour*, 2020, <who.int/publications/i/item/9789240015128>.

WHO, 'Every move counts towards better health – says WHO', 25 November 2020, <who.int/news/item/25-11-2020-every-move-counts-towards-better-health-says-who>.

Amy Adkins, 'Only one in 10 people possess the talent to manage', Gallup, 13 April 2015, <gallup.com/workplace/236579/one-people-possess-talent-manage.aspx>.

Steven Pressfield, *The War of Art: Break Through the Blocks and Win Your Inner Creative Battles*, Rugged Land, New York, 2012.

Index

$100 game, the 131
achievement 20-21
Achievers Workforce Institute
 163, 172
adaptability 112
advantage 17-27
airports 108, 135, 139, 191
alignment 190-192
alternative culture 9-11
Amazon 124
Anderson, Chris 23
Apple 57
Applewhite, Marshall 181
appreciation 152
aspirations 135-136
Atomic Habits 132
Aurecon 132-133
averages 135-136

Beaumont People 166-172
Beaumont, Nikki 166-172
behavioural conditioning 140
behaviours 96
—changing 132

—core 103-104
—defining 102
—observable 91-93
belief systems 184, 186
belonging 22-23
Bennett, Anne 119, 122, 123
Berkeley Culture Initiative 109,
 134, 191
Beth (interviewee) 69-72
Blanchard, Ken 172
Bond, Danielle 132
brand advocates 19
Brown, Brené 55
building culture 197-213
Bundaberg 5-6
Businessolver 56
buzz words 113-114

California State University,
 Chico 182
celebration 141-142, 154, 161-180
Chand, Dr Samuel 181
change 210-211
charisma 184-185

Chick-Fil-A 132
choice 197-198
chunking down 79-80, 100, 101
chunking up 79-81, 83-84
Cisco 93-99
clarification 87-106
clarity 207-208
Clear, James 132
Clifton, Jim 42
CliftonStrengths 75, 129
coaching 151
collaboration 198-199
Comer, James 93-99
communication 13-14, 88,
    107-127, 199-200
conditions, work 25
confidence 44
conflict 6-7, 75-76, 147-148
confrontation 141, 143-160
conscious culture 93-99
control 184, 192
Cook, Tim 57
Cooke, Robert 36
Corrie (interviewee) 8-11, 14,
    133
counselling 88-89
Covey, Sean 129
COVID-19 10-11, 21, 24-26, 51,
    55, 71-72, 139, 206
creativity 23-24
Crucial Conversations 144
cults 181-195
Culture Champions 203-210
culture charters 169-170
culture document 70-72

culture killers 198-201
curiosity 58-59, 82
Curzan, Anne 120

Davey, Liane 145
Dawkins, Richard 115
definition 89-91
definition dilemma, the 30-37
Deloitte 33
Democratic Workers Party in
    California 182
differences 3-15
directions 47-48
disappointment 67-68
disproportionate energy 132
disruption 20-21, 25-26, 56, 108
Dolan, Gabrielle (Ral) 118-120,
    123
Dredge, Rohan 164
Dvorak, Nate 19

Edelman 53
Edmondson, Amy 21-22
effort 130
Ek, Daniel 116
Eletto, Tory 67
empathy 56-58
employee attraction and retention
    18-20
engagement surveys 98-99
Entain 43
*Escaping Utopia: Growing Up in
    a Cult, Getting Out, and Starting
    Over* 184
expectation 67-86, 200

fatigue 25
feedback 143-160, 199-200
Ferrari 8
Feynman, Richard P. 79
Flores, Karl Kristian 3
focus 129-138, 157
Formula 1 8
Forsyth, Brittany 87
From Strategy to Action: A Guide to Getting Shit Done in the Public Sector 131

Gallup 18-20, 24, 42, 53, 58, 74-75, 129, 145, 163, 173, 204
Gerzon, Mark 147-148
Ghobadian, Abby 17
Google 59-60, 116-117
Google Trends 1
government, local x
Grant, Adam 55
Great Ormond Street Hospital (GOSH) 7-8
Great Resignation, the 25-26
Gruenert, Steve 143
Guinness World Records 169

Haas School of Business 109
Hale–Bopp comet 182
Hanlon's Razor 146
Harter, Jim 42
HBR IdeaCast 22, 120
Heaven's Gate 181-182, 183
Heskett, James 36
Hessels, Marco 34

Huling, Jim 129
human resources 136

identity 25
impact of culture 18-25
inclusion 22-23, 72-73
influence 184
influencing culture 39-40, 42-43
innovation 23-24
integrity 119
intention 95
interpretation 88-89
iteration 186-188

jargon 114, 120
Johansson, Frans 7
Johnson, Spencer 172

Klotz, Dr Anthony C. 25
Kotter, John 36
Kouts, Jim 9

Lalich, Dr Janja 182-185, 187-191
language 34-35, 87-106, 123-125
Lead the Room: Communicate a Message That Counts in Moments That Matter xii, 51, 89, 124
leaders, characteristics of great 59, 155-158, 199, 203-210
leadership dilemma, the 37-44
Leading Edge, The 81-82
Lencioni, Patrick 56
Lincoln (mentor) 3, 202

Matrix, The 23
Maxwell, John C. 202
McChesney, Chris 129
McCrindle Research xiii
McHenry, David 52
McKay, Alicia 131
McKinsey 24
measuring success 46
memes 115-116
Microsoft Teams 110
middle manager xv
Miller, James Nathan 51
missing voice, the 61-62
motivation 45-46
Mottau, Dan 91-93, 210

Netflix 70, 124
Nike 52

O.C. Tanner 162, 173
O'Neill, Lisa 161
O'Regan, Nicholas 17
Off Ya Tree 9
Olympics 119-120, 122, 167
One Minute Manager, The 172
oneness 190-192
Oprah Winfrey Show, The 164

Pauls 197
Pavlov, Ivan 140
Pendell, Ryan 19
people leader xv-xvi
Phone Calls with Clever People
 7, 23

Pressfield, Steve 211
prioritisation 45, 129-138
problems with culture 29-49
problem-solving 58-59
profit 24
Project Aristotle 60
Project Oxygen 59
punctuality 155-156
PwC 21, 24

quality circles 187

Ransom, Holly 81-82
Real Communication: How to Be
 You and Lead True 119
recognition 161-180
research xii-xiii
resignations 25
resilience 188-190
responsibility 37-44
results 24-25
revenue 24
Richards, Nigel 107-108
rituals 97-99, 134-135
Robbins, Chuck 94
Robertson, Fiona 23
Rogers, Kenny 123
Rules of Belonging 23
running 51-52

safety 21-22, 59-61
sameness 190-192
San Diego 181
Sandberg, Sheryl 130

Schien, Edgar H. 36, 107
Schwartz, Barry 197
Scrabble 107-108
Selfish Gene, The 115
Senn, Larry 36
Sharpe, Jessica 43
Shopify 87
silence 145
skills dilemma, the 44-47
Slack 110
Society for Human Resource
  Management (SHRM) 42
Spotify 116, 123
Srivastava, Sameer B. 109-112,
  134, 191, 192-193
Stanford 110
Stanier, Michael Bungay 58
Stanley, Andy 124, 154
stories 121-123
storytelling 118-120
strategy 38-40, 45
success 207

Taipei Songshan Airport 139
Tassopoulos, Tim 132
Team Space 97-98
teams, characteristics of
  effective 60, 69, 96-97
teamwork 198-199
TED 23, 55
Thendro 9-12, 133
Ting Hsu 139
TOFU 115-116, 120

toxic culture 144-145, 181-195
training 44, 46-47, 209
transparency 207
trust 53-55, 200, 207

UK Department of Health 72-73
unity 190-192
University of California,
  Berkeley 109

validation 164
values 92-93
Verbeke, Willem 34
VitalSmarts 144
Volgering, Marco 34
vulnerability 55-56

Wallace, David Foster ix
Warrick, D.D. 178
Watkins, Michael D. 29
Weiner, Jeff 221
Whitaker, Todd 143
Wichita test 191
Wieck, Karl 124
Wigmore, John Henry 82
Winfrey, Oprah 164
Workforce Institute at UKG,
  the 54
WorkLife 55
World Health Organization 201

Ziglar, Zig 197
Zoom 110

Let's continue the conversation

This book is a beginning not an end. It's an invitation to begin a conversation that continues beyond the pages you hold in your hand. If you have found this book valuable in any way there are a number of ways to continue the conversation. I would love you to share your story with me. Whether it's a few lines or a few pages, I would be honoured to read how this book has impacted you or helped you become a better leader. You can email me directly at contact@shanemhatton.com.

I write regularly on leadership and communication as a helpful resource to an incredible community of people. You are invited to be a part of that community. You can join easily by visiting www. shanemhatton.com. There you will also find more information about my programs and ways we can do great work together. Finally, if this book has helped you, why not invest it into the life of a colleague, team member or friend and start a conversation with them.

I can't wait to continue the conversation with you.

Be better with business books

MAJOR STREET

We hope you enjoy reading this book. We'd love you to post a review on social media or your favourite bookseller site. Please include the hashtag #majorstreetpublishing.

Major Street Publishing specialises in business, leadership, personal finance and motivational non-fiction books. If you'd like to receive regular updates about new Major Street books, email info@majorstreet.com.au and ask to be added to our mailing list.

Visit majorstreet.com.au to find out more about our books (print, audio and ebooks) and authors, read reviews and find links to our Your Next Read podcast.

We'd love you to follow us on social media.

in linkedin.com/company/major-street-publishing

f facebook.com/MajorStreetPublishing

○ instagram.com/majorstreetpublishing

▸ @MajorStreetPub